Crossing the Unknown Sea

Also by David Whyte

Crossing the Unknown Sea

WORK AS A PILGRIMAGE OF IDENTITY

David Whyte

RIVERHEAD BOOKS

NEW YORK

2001

RIVERHEAD BOOKS
a member of
Penguin Putnam Inc.
375 Hudson Street
New York, NY 10014

Library of Congress Cataloging-in-Publication Data

Whyte, David.
Crossing the unknown sea : work as a pilgrimage of identity /
David Whyte.
p.   cm.
ISBN 1-57322-178-3
1. Work.   I. Title.
BJ1498 .W48   2001   00-046891
174—dc21

Printed in the United States of America

1   3   5   7   9   10   8   6   4   2

This book is printed on acid-free paper. ∞

Book design by Marysarah Quinn

A c k n o w l e d g m e n t s

To my wife, Leslie; her intelligent conversation on the subtle identities of work, her loving and patient companionship and her understanding of the travails of the writer were a constant strength to me. To my daughter Charlotte for her joyous infancy; long may she continue to interrupt the strange priorities of the adult world. To my son Brendan for his companionship in the mountains, his humor, and the long morning sleeps appropriate to his teenhood that allowed me to finish the book during our memorable holiday. To Edward Wates for the timeless friendship, the single malt whiskey, the long night walks in Oxford, and the close listening. To John O'Donohue, a poetic and imaginative brother, whose good and strengthening words during a scintillating literary weekend with our mothers set me to rights for the last stretch. To my mother and father, who figure largely in my inherited understanding of work. To Bennett White for his laughter and cheerful fortitude. To Val Morgan for excellent cooking, unsurpassable red wine, and the much-needed familial hospitality of Bovingdon. To Tony Morgan, whose encouraging early morning remarks greatly nourished a sense of promise in the manuscript. To my assistant Julie Quiring for her intelligent reading and acute comments on the first chapters. To Donna Humphreys for her resourceful and meticulous help with permissions. To Susan Petersen Kennedy, who hunted me out of the poetic undergrowth to write prose again. To my agent Ned

Leavitt, who carried the true spirit of the writer's intentions into his negotiations. And last, to my editor at Riverhead, Amy Hertz, who has a sure and intuitive understanding of the book struggling to be born from a writer's first imaginative stirrings. This book is far better for her astute and careful comments than anything I could have accomplished alone. All the above have contributed to whatever qualities the book may possess; its flaws and omissions are all my own.

FOR THREE LOVES:

Leslie,

Charlotte,

AND

Brendan.

You have set sail on another ocean
without star or compass
going where the argument leads
shattering the certainties of centuries.

—JANET KALVEN,
"Respectable Outlaw"

Contents

Pilgrimage

Beginnings

I

Courage and Conversation:

SETTING OUT WITH A FIRM PERSUASION

> *Then I asked: Does a firm persuasion that a thing is so, make it*
> *so? He replied: All poets believe that it does, and in ages of*
> *imagination this firm persuasion removed mountains; but many*
> *are not capable of a firm persuasion of anything.*
>
> —WILLIAM BLAKE
> *The Marriage of Heaven and Hell*

Work is a very serious matter in almost all respects, whether it is work in the shelter of our home or work in the big, wide, dangerous world. Through work, human beings earn for themselves and their families, make a difficult world habitable, and with imagination, create some meaning from what they do and how they do it. The human approach to work can be naïve, fatalistic, power-mad, money-grubbing, unenthusiastic, cynical, detached, and obsessive. It can also be selflessly mature, revelatory and life giving; mature in its long-reaching effects, and life giving in the way it gives back to an individual or society as much as it has taken. Almost always it is both, a sky full of light and dark, with all the varied weather of an individual life blowing through it.

There is no hiding from work in one form or another. Under

the great sky of our endeavors we live our lives, growing we hope, through its seasons toward some kind of greater perspective. Any perspective is dearly won. Maturity and energy in our work is not granted freely to human beings but must be adventured and discovered, cultivated and earned. It is the result of application, dedication, an indispensable sense of humor, and above all a never-ending courageous conversation with ourselves, those with whom we work, and those whom we serve. It is a long journey; it calls on both the ardors of youth and the perspectives of a longer view. It is achieved through a lifelong pilgrimage.

William Blake, that unstoppable creator, as both poet and engraver seemed to have a direct and conversational relationship with the wellsprings of work. Over a lifetime he exhibited a continual inspiration, a profound vision and an indomitable ability, despite his poverty, to follow through with the tiniest details of his art. Blake called his sense of dedication a *firm persuasion*. To have a firm persuasion in our work—to feel that what we do is right for ourselves and good for the world at the exactly same time—is one of the great triumphs of human existence. We do feel, when we have work that is challenging and enlarging and that seems to be doing something for others, as if, in Blake's words, we could move mountains, as if we could call the world *home;* and for a while, in our imaginations, no matter the small size of our apartment, we dwell in a spacious house with endless horizons.

"*My fingers Emit sparks of fire with Expectation of my future labours,*" said the passionate Blake, in a letter promising plenty of hard work to his patron, Hayley. He was speaking from a felt sense of fulfillment and from the very last part of the eighteenth century, an age when our Western ideas of work were going through enormous change, an age when the factory was born, and production in and for itself was first conceived as an imaginative good. But Blake stood firm amid it all in his approach to work and in his writings, saying essentially *nothing* had changed. Factory or farm, individuals needed a sense of belonging in their work, a conversation with something larger than themselves, a felt participation, and a touch of spiritual fulfillment and the mysterious generative nature of that fulfillment. Blake might have said that they needed a conversation with the angels. Earning and providing were all very well, but once the basics were met, human beings naturally turned their inward and outward eyes to greater horizons.

Whether fulfillment lasts for a month or for a lifetime, most of us would not complain of its appearance in our lives however long or short its stay. If we cannot have Blake's lifelong experience of wonder and inspiration through our labors, we will take just the merest touch now and again. Some have experienced fulfillment for only a few brief hours early on in their work lives and then measured everything, secretly, against it since. Some have felt eager and engaged by their work for years and then walked into their office one fine morning to find their enthusiasms gone, their energies spent, their imaginations engaged in secret ways, elsewhere.

To have a *firm persuasion,* to set out boldly in our work, is to make a pilgrimage of our labors, to understand that the consummation of work lies not only in what we have done, but who we have become while accomplishing the task. To see life and work as a pilgrimage is not a strategy for increased production (though by understanding the wellsprings of human creativity, there is every chance it might happen); it does not mean that we can lay out our careers in precise stages, clearly and concisely, as to when, where and how everything should happen. All of our great artistic and religious traditions take equally great pains to inform us that we must never mistake a good *career* for good work. Life is a creative, intimate and unpredictable conversation if it is nothing else, spoken or unspoken, and our *life* and our *work* are both the result of the particular way we hold that passionate conversation. In Blake's sense, a *firm persuasion,* was a form of *self-knowledge;* it was understood as a result, an outcome, a bounty that came from paying close attention to an astonishing world and the way each of us is made differently and uniquely for that world.

FAITH AND WORK

Blake saw the great powers of life working on us like a kind of permanent gravity field, the currents of life acting and pulling upon us according to our particular heft and spiritual weight, our makeup and our nature. These currents surround us and inform us whether we are in the kitchen or in the office, in the woods alone, or crowded in a downtown elevator. To have a *firm persuasion,* according to Blake, we must come to know these currents that surround us in an intimate way and build a kind of faith from the directional movement that results from a close conversation with these elements. Almost like a sail conversing with the wind, every sail will respond differently to the elements according to its shape and the vessel it propels. And the response of the sail, with a steady hand at the tiller, creates movement and direction. In this conversation no one can get stuck for long; as an individual, you simply need to present some surface area to life. In Woody Allen's words: *Just show up;* then it is only a question of direction.

Showing up for work is difficult. You would think *not* showing up would be impossible for living, breathing human beings, but we know enough of ourselves on a bleak Monday morning, or certain co-workers of a bad day, to realize that as human beings, we are the one part of creation that can refuse to be itself. Our bodies can be present in our work, but our hearts, minds, and imaginations can be placed firmly in neutral or engaged elsewhere.

FAITH AND DOUBT

Sometimes our hiding from others has been so successful that we can no longer even find ourselves when we want to. We feel submerged, heavy, immovable, stuck forever in the mud of our own making. I think of the patterns of air that circulate around a plane's wing, lifting even the deadliest, heaviest part of us up and away, off the ground. Blake must have believed that every human being has access to these metaphorical aerodynamics; he drew figures depicting the dramas of human existence, people flying, falling, coming to earth or spiralling upward. He thought of the artist as a whole man or woman, someone with utter faith in the conversation, alert to the forces that stream around us. To waken this inner artist, we must assume a certain shape that puts us in conversation with the elements; we must cultivate a kind of faith in the moving energies around us and the way they to come to our aid, give us lift, no matter our circumstances or difficulties.

If the Sun and Moon should doubt,
They'd immediately go out.

Blake said, sure of the brilliant and reflective nature of faith. Not that any life is free from doubt, especially when it comes to our work and the places we work. Many's the time we gaze into the mirror in the course of a long work life and see our own faces shaded and eclipsed by a complete loss of connection with our striving. The eyes dimmed, the professional smile false and forced. We pick up the phone and make the call, though we have nothing to say.

Whatever doubt we have, Blake asks us to put that doubt in conversation with grander, more eternal, more essential parts of ourselves. Underneath the face, underneath the surface professionalism, underneath the brief obituary in the paper, there are forces grander than any individual human life at play. To lose contact with these forces is to lose a real sense of living, and especially of living a life we can call our own. Suicide, literal or metaphorical, is the loss of conversation with these forces. Any life, and any life's work, is a hidden journey, a secret code, deciphered in fits and starts. The details only given truth by the whole, and the whole dependent on the detail.

I I

The Mountain Farm:

A STRANGER AT THE DOOR

Years ago, in my early twenties, on a mountainside in North Wales, at the far end of Cwm Pennant, I found myself alone, lighting a fire in the grate of my friends' farmhouse, waiting in vain for their imminent arrival. I had walked the long Welsh miles up the wet road, in rain and cold wind, but no car had passed me in the darkening winter light the whole length of the valley. I had hurried past the old tower in the woods that gave this remote place a strange fairy-tale aspect, then struck up the narrow hill lane and emerged on the ridge. Ahead of me, I could see the ancient farmhouse that always seemed, at first sight, to grow out of the mountain.

I was cold, and I looked forward, in that freezing wind, to joining my friends, to their warm welcome and the hiss of a kettle. But the farmhouse was dark and silent as I walked through the gate. That day the house seemed to be waiting for someone in its slate-gray stillness, but there was no answer to my knock. I finally pushed the door open and went in. The kitchen was empty, cold, and lightless, as if the walls were used to the coming and goings of whole generations and one day of human absence was nothing in the span of centuries; but I was glad to be there, even alone. At least I would be dry in the midst of this arriving storm. I listened to the wind now beginning to tear at the trees, and shook off my coat and the rain. Here, alone in the place it seemed as if the farmhouse had taken on the essential character of a timeless and sheltering roof. It had been here for centuries, immovable, and today it seemed both generous and indifferent to me, a lone stranger waiting for his friends.

I entered the living room, saw the empty grate in the fireplace, and looked out of the window onto a familiar landscape: the lowering valley shadowed by cloud, the cold, blue, snow-rimed hills, all announcing the coming of a very wet and very Welsh winter night. Beyond the mouth of the valley the dark slate of the sea surged ominously, lit by the final slants of evening light flung across its surface.

Looking for a Vision

I couldn't help thinking, looking over the grand display of mountain and sea, that I was looking for an equally grand perspective for my coming work life. I needed, in Blake's words, a firm persuasion, a conversation with something larger than my own personal hopes for a career. I was about to step out into the world from the shelter of my studies for what seemed like a forbidding journey. There were no jobs available in my chosen field of marine zoology, and thousands of unemployed graduates at that time to tell you that your dreams were to no avail.

In short, I was in the difficult place most of us find ourselves whether we are beginning biologists or bankers, aspiring academics or hopeful carpenters. I had a vague image inside me of what I really wanted to do—which at that time, in my single, young existence, was to live in some marvelously exotic place studying the life of the oceans—and an even vaguer idea of how I should go about it. Looking back, I realize now that I had far more than I could appreciate. To have even the least notion of what we want to do in life is an enormous step in and of itself, and it is silver, gold, the moon, and the stars to those who struggle for the merest glimmer of what they want or what they are suited to.

One of the keys to any possible happiness in work must be the little self-knowledge it takes to know what we desire in life, how we are made, and how we belong to the rest of the world. But at this stage in my life, just prior to stepping out into the big world, I felt I was losing any faith in myself and what I wanted. I felt old, precious images of a work and a life that I had nurtured since childhood slipping through my open fingers.

WORK, WORK, WORK

Work is difficulty and drama, a high-stakes game in which our identity, our esteem, and our ability to provide are mixed inside of us in volatile, sometimes explosive ways. We may have a difficult but outwardly calm day at work, and then find ourselves bawling at family members the moment we get through the door. We may be unhappy in our marriage but find our inchoate despair erupts only with co-workers. "Sara had a meltdown," we say, describing our supervisor's tirade, or "John finally lost it," remembering yesterday's confrontation. We describe dramas in the workplace as though we were outlining alchemical reactions or intuiting the ability of individuals to both find and then lose themselves in the midst of seemingly hardheaded decisions.

Work is where we can make ourselves; work is where we can break ourselves. It is a making and an unmaking that can ultimately never be measured by money alone. In work we can indeed, and in a moment, build or ruin our fiscal fortunes, or we can slowly and imperceptibly, over long years, destroy the inner complexion of our character. Sometimes to our despair, we know instinctively that work is never done. At its worst we are Sisyphus, pushing the boulder over the last incline only to see it fall back and away, out of our grasp, to the very bottom of the slope, to be pushed back up with the same despairing effort the following Monday morning.

At its best, work seems never-ending only because, like life, it is a pilgrimage, a journey in which we progress not only through the world but through stages of understanding. Good work, done well for the right reasons and with an end in mind, has always been a sign, in most human traditions, of an inner and outer maturity. Its achievement is celebrated as an individual triumph and a gift to our societies. A very hard-won arrival.

Seen in the light of a pilgrim's journey, work takes on a greater significance than merely paying the bills and keeping the ever-present wolf from the door. With something larger in mind, something yet to be fully imagined, something to be looked for, then the hazards and the hopes, the trepidation and the triumphs of work are magnified and given import and meaning.

It is very hard to say no to work. We may courageously resign, take a sabbatical, or retire to a simpler, more rustic existence, but then we are engaged in inner work, or working on ourselves, or just chopping wood. Work means application, explication, expectation. There is almost no life a human being can construct for themselves where they are not wrestling with something difficult, something that takes a modicum of work. The only possibility seems to be the ability of human beings to choose good work. At its simplest, good work is work that makes sense, and that grants sense and meaning to the one who is doing it and to those affected by it.

The stakes in good work are necessarily high. Our competence may be at stake in ordinary, unthinking work, but in good work that is a heartfelt expression of ourselves, we necessarily put our very identities to hazard. Perhaps it is because we know, in the end, we *are* our gift to others and the world. Failure in truly creative work is not some mechanical breakdown but the prospect of a failure in our very essence, a kind of living death. Little wonder we often choose the less vulnerable, more familiar approach, that places work mostly in terms of provision. If I can reduce my image of work to just a job I have to do, then I keep myself safely away from the losses to be endured in putting my heart's desires at stake.

To view work as a pilgrimage is to put our hearts' desires to hazard, because by merely setting out, we have told ourselves that there is something bigger and better, or even smaller and better—above all, something more life giving—that awaits us in our work, and we are going to seek it. We look around to see what we have for the journey and find at bottom that we possess only intuitions and imagination. We look for courage and as yet find little of it.

FINDING THE COURAGE TO BEGIN

We say to ourselves that we need more than ordinary courage, but really there is no ordinary courage. Either we are courageous or we are not. But the key is in the word *courage* itself. The word *courage* arises from the old French *cuer,* meaning heart. To be courageous means at bottom to be heartfelt. To begin with we take only those steps which we can do in a heartfelt fashion and then slowly increase our stride as we become familiar with the direct connection between our passion and our courage. Without some kind of fire at the center of the conversation, a sense of journey through work, life becomes just another strategic game plan, a way of pulling wool over the eyes of reality while we get our own way.

Once we have kindled our desire for something better in our work, we have immediately raised the stakes. Once we have taken the first tentative steps toward worthwhile creative work, we have brought to life embers inside us that would signal some kind of inner death should they then go out. In taking our work seriously as an expression of our belonging, we hazard our most precious— sometimes our seemingly most fragile hopes and dreams, in a world that is more often than not associated with a harsh and destructive bottom line.

Alone in that cottage, all those years ago, I had begun to shiver not only with the cold of a Welsh mountain winter, but with an awful sense that I was suddenly about to play by different rules. That the inner light of youthful imaginings might be smothered by hard-bitten adult notions of work, inherited generation after generation.

There are deep wells of loss, bitterness and exploitation when it comes to our human history around work. I realized that these wells could erupt and flood over any youthful individual hopes, whatever age I was, and drown them. The world of work I was about to confront was a mighty inherited sea of hard-won experience, and I was just a small vessel coasting for the moment among its inshore inlets and bays.

A STRANGER AT THE DOOR

I set to lighting the fire, carefully nestling the coals among the burning kindling and had just finally brought it to life when I heard a knock at the old weather-beaten door. I opened it to find another stranger to the house, drenched by the same walk up the valley and looking, as I was, for my friends. I invited him to the fire, and as the evening slipped by, and he began to dry out, we found ourselves overcoming our initial wariness, and the strangeness of the situation: two unknown quantities in an unknown home, beginning to tell each other, as strangers do, a little of our life stories. We covered a lot of ground very quickly, but as I was soon to find out, in the first round of conversation, he held back from the central drama.

As we moved on from our brief introductions, our conversation roved over the particular atmosphere and character of the wooded valley of Cwm Pennant directly below our window. We both loved the mountains and valleys of Snowdonia, and I was glad to talk with someone who shared the same enthusiasm for this rugged corner of Wales, but his was no ordinary appreciation. I was struck by his detailed knowledge of woodlands, trees, and animals. Not only his knowledge but his storyteller's ability to articulate and reframe the natural world around us so that I began to glimpse it again in his words as if for the first time. Despite my own hard studies in biology, I found in listening to him that I was beginning to see it all again with new eyes. As the hours passed, I began to feel that this stranger was a very singular man, both in his work and his way with words. He was both a landscape gardener and a self-taught expert in the study of woodlands. His work also had some literal ground under it. He managed planting projects all over England and Wales.

ASKING THE QUESTION

It is always a privilege to see in one person, knowledge, imagination and articulation combined, and a double privilege to be in conversation alone with that synergy of talents. I couldn't help but warm to him, and I couldn't help but open the small bottle of brandy I had brought to share with my friends. I was sure now they would never arrive that night. As I opened the bottle, I asked him how he had come to all this knowledge, and more to the point of my curiosity, how had he come to do the work he loved? I found myself telling him, as I would not have told many closer to me, that I felt stopped at a crossroads, looking for direction, unsure of my next steps. I told him I was beginning to feel a few icy tendrils of cynicism around what work might actually mean to most of the adult world, and with a long work life still ahead of me, I wanted to know what it took to find a life and a work such as he had found, a work into which you could really put your heart and soul.

"So, what took you into all this?" I said as innocently as I could, pouring and holding up to him in the firelight, a half-filled glass.

He took a deep breath, and at the same time, if I remember correctly, a swift, warming draught of the brandy, and said,

"Do you really want to know?"

Did I want to know? I looked at him, I looked at the brandy. I said that we had plenty of time and as it was now approaching midnight, little chance of our mutual friends coming back to disturb us. He nodded back quickly in agreement and started straight in, the beauties of North Wales faded quickly in his first words.

"I was entirely and utterly desperate," he said. "Living in a dingy North London flat with people I couldn't trust and who couldn't trust me. That's a story in itself, how I got to that point, with those kind of people in that kind of place, but I was one of them. I was a druggie, a dodo, a complete addict." He looked me in the eye to see how this knowledge registered with me. I could see that he wasn't worried what I would think, he was looking to see if I was worth the telling of the tale.

"I was at the end of my tether and ready to end it all. I sat on that scuffed floor, looking at the open twelfth-floor window in my flat, coming to terms with the sheer bloody awfulness of my life and the way I had made a complete mess of it all. I felt sure that everything had abandoned me, and because of that I had abandoned everything in turn, including the little faith I had in myself. "

"That brandy," I said. "Perhaps we shouldn't?"

"Thank you," he said, with an airy wave of his hand, "and don't worry, I can take this now or leave it; it was much harder stuff than this that brought me to the point of wanting to jump out of that window."

He paused for effect, and the wind now howling outside the walls seemed to emphasize the silence he had created in the room.

"Jump?"

"Jump. I got myself onto the window ledge with every intent of going through with it. I wanted to jump. It was a bloody long way to the ground, at least high enough to do the job, but I was too weak. I barely fed myself at the time, and there was this huge unkempt flower box across the whole length of the window."

"You obviously didn't do it."

"Not for the want of trying. I couldn't get over it. I still can't get over it. I've never been so humiliated. I couldn't even kill myself properly. The edges of the box were so high, I ended up with my chin in the mud and knees under the box. I have to laugh now, but it wasn't much of a laughing matter then. My sweater was caught on a nail, my knees wouldn't come over the inside of the box, and I had a cramp in my leg. I ended up sprawled across the wooden trough with the rain falling on me, my hands in the dirt, the tears running down my face in absolute frustration. I must have looked a sight, but nobody saw me. I suppose at that time I wouldn't have cared if they had; the great thing was, I just gave up. There was nothing waiting for me back through that window, in that awful room, so I just lay there for the longest time, my arms out and my face down in the mud."

A TURN OF THE TIDE

"Facedown in the mud, something happened I hadn't felt for years. I think that there are some experiences you can only crawl into on your hands and knees in order to understand them. A psy-chiatrist once told me that suicide is not one event but a confluence of many happening all at once, and all of the conditions have to be right for the person to go through with it. First of all, you need despair, and yet strangely enough, while you are in despair the sec-ond thing you need is the will to do it, which, when you think about it, is a strange combination. Third, you need the weapon; fourth, you need to be alone; and fifth and last, you need the opportunity. Stuck in that planting box, I had lost my weapon; looking down at the soil in that box, I lost my despair. And suddenly I didn't feel alone anymore. When the passion for ending myself had receded along with all those necessary conditions, I felt incredibly peaceful spread-eagled on the cliff edge of that muddy box. There was nowhere else to go and I was at least halfway out of the home I hated, halfway toward something better. It came over me, sudden, like. That's suicide, you know: You get stuck and it's time to move on, but you make the simple mistake of thinking you have to kill yourself to do it.

"Suddenly I felt as if everything was in its proper place. I couldn't quite believe it. I had literally opened a window and taken a little breath of freedom and entered a stillness I hadn't felt since I was a child. You know, when you could look out of your window at the street and everything seemed to be waiting for you. As if there was a special kind of invitation waiting for you, and you alone, and you just had to listen hard to hear it. Well, there I was again. Oh, I hadn't felt like that for years. First I was weeping with frustration, and then I was weeping because there was nowhere I needed to go. I was having a good cry for that young fellah inside me, waiting all those years to hear his name being called.

"It had been raining nonstop for days, part of why I wanted to chuck myself out the window, I suppose. I looked down and noticed that the rain had been running into one end of the flower box and carved a little river valley the whole length of the window. There was a miniature world right beneath my nose, a little Montana in that scene beneath me. On the banks of the tiny river, in the brown mud, there were green plants and shoots growing along its edge. It was the only world I had at that moment, so I took a good long look at it. Sometime in the next hour or so of lying there in my new-found peace, I began to mold the muddy earth into little hills and banks with my hands. I started to form little side branches of the river, and I began to lift some plants out carefully and put them in different places.

"I must have lain there, wet through, working the ground with my hands, for a very long time, but for the first time in a very long time I had a glimmer, just a glimmer, of something I could do, something I could literally get my hands on. I felt as if God had looked at me again, and in that hour in the rain, in that tiny little world, halfway out of a twelfth-floor window, I had looked back at Him. Not that I'm formally religious or anything, but something had given me back an old memory, a sense of creation, a way back into the world.

"I had my hands in the soil and I was molding the ground on a small scale the way I do now on a larger scale. I was landscaping, damn it. I was working the ground of my future life. That's how I got here. I went back through the window, into that flat; I washed myself without thinking and with a determination I hadn't felt for months; I went straight out. I fixed my eyes right on the ground, walked straight past my local dealer on the corner and knocked loudly on the door of a friend. He wouldn't believe my little epiphany but he was a good friend and he helped me check me into detox. When I came out at the other end I enrolled in a landscape course. A year later I moved to Wales. He believed me then, and more important, *I* believed me. It was the first courageous thing I'd done in years. I've never touched the hard stuff again—no, no need for it now, just a glass like this now and again; I have my work and I don't want any other life but the one I have."

I must have been staring at him with my mouth open, because he leaned forward, looked me directly in the eye, and said, "We all have our own ground to work, you know. You have yours, too. You just have to find out what it is. But you know what? It is right on the edge of yourself. At the cliff edge of life. That's the edge you go to. Put yourself in conversation with that edge no matter how frightening it seems. Look down over that edge. It's a bit terrifying to begin with but then you'll recognize a bit of territory that you can work, something you can step out onto. It was there all the time for me, when I look back, just on the other side of a too, too familiar window, out of which I had *not* been looking."

LOOKING OUT TO SEA

Our mutual friends never appeared at the farmhouse that night, and we were left with each other and the remnants of the half bottle of brandy until we fell asleep in opposing armchairs, just as the moon was beginning to show itself after the storm. I remember the conversation as a kind of gifted revelation, as if in that listening I had been rejoined with familiar but forgotten voices essential to my own life and work. I had listened so intently that I felt as if I had lain in that flower box along with him.

In the wee hours of that night, by the fire, on a rainy Welsh mountainside, I began to work the clay of my own life again, to mold the territory of my own belonging. In the intimacy of the stranger's story and the conversation that followed, I found myself beginning to articulate and reshape my history and felt newly emboldened for the waiting future that might lie ahead of me beyond that winter night.

By dawn, I was staring out over the far sea, involved in a strange inversion of the stranger's experience, for I felt as if *I* was new ground and the vast sea was reaching into my contained territory and molding and shaping a future life. All the hours of the early morning, I looked out, feeling a kind of magnetism to that far windswept ocean, as if aware of the forces in my future that would draw me into my work, whatever form it would take, over the horizons and unknown seas to the west.

MEMORY AND MAGIC

Looking back to that mountain farmhouse in the early 1970s from our present brave new technological world, I feel as if I am gazing on a primary, almost mythological layer of experience. The encounter in the farmhouse seems storybook, other-worldly, outlined and dramatized by memory and the pivotal nature of the encounter. Work centers so much on technology today, and the imagination mediated through technology, that it is easy to forget that the Dow Jones, the NASDAQ, the hardware, the software and the shareware are all meant to be good servants to the individual human soul's desire to belong to the world. Not that it was any easier to find good work in the early seventies than it is now. Quite the opposite. I am gazing, I suppose, into a period of youthful aspiration in my own history, when my desires and my needs of the world were more touchable and urgent. But the more I look back into those youthful energies, the more certain I am that they are needed in all the stages of pilgrimage in a work life. We need, at every stage in our journey through work, to be in conversation with our desire for something suited to us and our individual natures.

To my mind, one of the great disciplines of any human life is the discipline of memory, of remembering what is essential in the midst of our business and busyness. The human soul thrives on and finds courage from the difficult intimacies of belonging. But it is almost as if, afraid of those primary intimacies, we have unconsciously created a work world so secondary, so complex, and so busy and bullied by surface forces that embroiled in those surface difficulties, we have the perfect busy excuse not to wrestle with the more essential difficulties of existence, the difficulties of finding a work and a life suited to our individual natures; the difficulties that would lead us to an older, intimate, and more human sense of belonging. In the farmhouse all those years ago, I stumbled into conversational intimacy with a stranger and felt the whole course of my life pivot in the encounter.

A MIDNIGHT CONVERSATION

In writing *Crossing the Unknown Sea,* I have attempted to re-create that special and privileged intimacy which occurs in the sudden encounter between strangers. A time when paths cross at exactly the moment when both writer and reader are ready for a greater perspective. A moment when both might be ready to know something of the territory through which they have passed and a glimpse of the unknown future which might lie ahead.

Crossing the Unknown Sea is meant to be an exploration and a midnight conversation, a look at our present vision of work and our ability to reimagine ourselves; a sea voyage into both our inherited notions of what work means to us and our experiences and intuitions of what lies over the horizon. A reminder that work is not a static endpoint or a mere exercise in providing, but a journey and a pilgrimage in which the core elements of our being are tested in the world.

Whether it be the Berlin Wall, apartheid, the bad old coercive Soviet system, or our own bad old coercive business systems, it seems that any foundations not now built on the realities of human relationship are being swept away by the forces of our time. In the same way, our notions of work are undergoing an enormous sea change, and because of that, our workplaces are themselves being worked on, molded and often scoured away by the same enormous tidal forces. We are moving from a familial, parent-child relationship in the workplace to an adult-adult relationship with our organizations, with all of the shock, difficulties, triumphs, and fears that entails. Unknown hands and as yet barely articulated tidal forces, are molding and scouring not only the ground on which we stand but the very shape of our identities.

Crossing the Unknown Sea hopes not only to chart the journey into work itself and our present sense of power and powerlessness, but to offer something of a journey, an arrival, and, if we are lucky, a little insight through its poetry, its memories, and its stories. All good storytelling is reshaped by the listening and attentive imagination. This book is an invitation to an imaginative conversation about life and work. In the attentive ear of the reader is the echo of the reader's own story, joined invisibly to the conversation.

Like the stranger I met that night on the mountainside, we mold the clay and ground of our lives and the territory of our work every day by what we do and how we do it. At times, many of us find ourselves hovering over precipitous heights, wondering if we should end it all—literally, like my mysterious friend, or metaphorically, by leaving our present work and its seeming entrapment. No matter, work in one form or another awaits us, whatever step we take, and probably, by its everlasting presence, even after death. Work, after all, at its best, is one of the great human gateways to the eternal and the timeless.

In work we are constantly attempting to remember ourselves and reimagine ourselves at the same time. We change ourselves and our world every day by the way we are on the phone, in the office cubicle, or across the carpenter's workbench. We may find our sense of belonging through investing millions in a millisecond in a myriad of countries, or more slowly by investing our time in a cluttered city office working with the local dispossessed. Wherever we work, we need courage both to remember what we are about and, according to the tenor of our times, reimagine ourselves while we are doing it. We are not alone in this endeavor but secretly joined to all those who struggle out loud where we have not yet begun to speak or, when publicly, we are loud and vociferous, to those who labor painfully and secretly beside us. We are joined especially to those who have come before us.

We are immensely privileged even to inquire about the meaning of our work. Many of our ancestors pined for good work as they would for a lover, and remained unrequited and stricken by want. Many of our ancestors died while working in dangerous or desperate conditions. Some left good work and found none to replace it. A few, a very few, left little, crossed oceans, and found abundance beyond hope. Others worked hard or traveled to new shores and dutifully sacrificed for their sons and daughters, while their hearts and minds were elsewhere, their own dreams unfulfilled, their innermost selves left high and dry, disappointed by time's fleeting tide. Whatever our inheritance of work in this life, we are only the apex of innumerable lives of endeavor and sacrifice. Where we have come from, the struggles of our parents, our ancestral countries, their voyages, and hardships are immensely important.

This book is meant to breathe upon and ignite the embers of our own memory and our own courage. In it, I hope to bring the powers of the imagination to bear on our present vexing, strategic questions about work and to call upon a deep, shared memory of the greater story of which we constantly forget we are a part. It is meant to get below our present preoccupation with the Dow Jones and the NASDAQ and begin an invisible conversation with all those who have gone before us and those who will inherit what we make of ourselves. It is, for the most part, a personal story, and as I have spent much of my life wrestling with unknowns, it is meant to be a dedication to that unknown. Our great hope, in wrestling with that unknown we must learn to call our life and our work, is to find a way to call on our courage for all the unknowns yet to come. I wrote this book based on my perception that at the threshold of our new century, we are attempting to gather whatever courage we have dormant in our hearts, individually and collectively, for a great journey across a difficult and unknown sea.

M i d   O c e a n

III

At the Cliff Edge of Life:

FROM POWERLESSNESS TO PARTICIPATION

I awoke to a different rhythm, a recognizably changed sway and catch of the boat's movement. As I opened my eyes, I felt a sudden subliminal terror. I knew immediately that the boat was moving free, at the mercy of the waves, under no human control. I felt instinctively the spectral loom of the land very near to us, and I heard a deep, muffled, booming sound which set my blood to freeze. I looked across and saw our new replacement captain asleep. I leapt out of my bunk and ran in a frenzy up the ladder to the cockpit. My first view was of last night's anchorage, two good sea miles to the stern and a vast gulf of choppy water between us and it. I looked quickly over my shoulder and swore out loud; the lava cliff shadowed everything, the tip of the mast swaying just feet from the outward curving wall. Beneath it, the waves were sounding off the rock and throwing spray over the boat. Even as I looked, the boat was beginning to turn sideways on, the mast rising toward the curving roof of the cliff.

A moment later we were front on again, the bow lifting toward the rock. I looked madly for the lay of the trailing anchor line and saw it mercifully free of the propeller. A quick twist of the oil key, a stab of the button, and the engine coughed into life; then a mist of diesel fumes, a moment of unspeakable fear beneath the unholy roof of the cliff as the bow reared toward that implacable solidity, and I flattened the lever back into reverse. The bow rail seemed to freeze forever on its rise, then it dropped, fell off, and retreated from the cliff; the stern shot suddenly backwards, the deathly cliff receded, the world returned swiftly to sanity again, and the captain bounded from below.

A mere eighteen months had passed since my encounter with the stranger high on a Welsh mountain and already I was on the far side of the world, farther than my imagination could have carried me that gray morning as I had looked out over the Irish Sea. The determination forged by my encounter with the stranger in the farmhouse seemed to have shifted the wind round in my favor, and I had graduated, weathered the gloomy job prospects, and, with good fortune favoring the newly brave, landed myself a plum job as a naturalist guide in the Galapagos islands.

I was right bang on the equator, in the Pacific Ocean, 700 miles from the South American coast, in the Mecca of biologists, living and working aboard the *Bronzewing,* a handsome forty-eight-foot sloop that had become my very movable home. Galapagos was everything a naturalist might dream of: exotic one-of-a-kind species above and below water, and the lingering glamour of Darwin's brief passage still shimmering in the air despite the 140 years since his going. Like the young Darwin who had arrived here electric with excitement, I felt I had my work now, and my direction; but no work or career can be a steady, laid-out progression. All in this garden was not completely rosy, and it was certainly no paradise familiar to the human eye.

THE SHOCK OF THE REAL

Though I had a dream job, I was suffering a kind of culture shock. Not the shock of encountering an unfamiliar human culture but the profound, shattering impact of looking nature straight in the face. I had encountered in Galapagos a culture that did not seem to include the human at all. For most of human history, these islands have remained undiscovered, and we are but recent visitors to Galapagos. As a species, we are youngsters in this very old world, and I was young, too, just in my early twenties. I found myself prone to the loneliness of this new world of ocean rocks and strange animals. I had come to study nature in all its glory, yet a secret portion of me found Galapagos in its raw form intensely frightening. Everywhere I went, I saw animals living and dying according to some other mercy than my human mind could stand. It all seemed to paint a world in which there was no immunity or hiding place for anything from the great cycles of life and death. This incident beneath the lava cliff was everything I had been anticipating for months in my secret fears.

Though we profess to love nature, we like it packaged according to our human desires. We do not look too hard at the world for fear of what we will find there. On the threshold of this new world, I was no exception. I found Galapagos intensely disturbing. The natural world unmediated by society is no picturesque, environmental idea but a raw force in which human beings often seem to participate on sufferance. Young as I was in Galapagos, I began to touch an exposed nerve in human experience: the sense that there is something larger in the world than mere human priorities. Whatever work I was doing, something larger, more frightening, with a different order of priorities was moving in parallel. Something that encompassed a grander and more difficult universe than my career goals.

NATURE, FORTUNE, AND FEAR

There is a long connection between the way we stand in fear of the natural world and the way we have used work as a bastion against the wilder, nonhuman forces of existence. Societally and individually, whatever we say on the surface, we are afraid of nature, and rightly so. Humans work hard and build imaginatively, generation after generation. Then, as Camille Paglia says, "Let nature shrug, and all is in ruin." Venezuelan shorelines disintegrate in torrential downpours. Industrious Kobe's concrete overpasses fall in a tremor as if pushed by a petulant child, and even now, vast shelves of Antarctic ice threaten to float off and melt in our warming seas. We hear the news and ignore it all, but underneath, some old human imagination is stirred. "Get a good job," a parent says, meaning "Get a safe job." As if, over the years they have learned the wicked, veering manner of the winds that blow through life in their unmerciful ways; but also, they are passing on, parent to child, a fear bred into our human bones of that dark outer wind's howling, pushing presence. The same wind that howled outside the farmhouse that night in Wales. The same winds that blew us onto the lava cliff from our anchorage. Work provides safety. To define work in other ways than safety is to risk our illusions of immunity in the one organized area of life where we seem to keep nature and the world at bay.

THE EDGE OF NECESSITY

In work, it has always taken courage to follow a unique and individual path exactly, because making our own path takes us off the path, in directions which seem profoundly unsafe. A pilgrimage into the night and the night wind. The territory through which we must travel to make a life for ourselves is always more difficult than we could first imagine; it takes us to the cliff edges of life. The amusing part is that you can spend years preparing for the possibility of falling *off* the cliff and then find yourself suddenly *under* the cliff, approaching it from another, equally terrifying direction.

Finding a work to which we can dedicate ourselves always calls for some kind of courage, some form of heartfelt participation. It needs courage because the intrinsic worth of work lies in the fact that it connects us to larger, fiercer worlds where we are forced to remember first priorities. The farm laborer knows the toil that literally puts bread on the table. The police officer knows firsthand the invisible line between order and disorder in society. I remember a recent dinner conversation with a water utility executive who had been in the midst of a massive Turkish earthquake. Awake night after night, doing work that was not part of his official job description, he and his team brought water, medicines, and supplies to bereft, panicking communities. Once the crisis was past, he wondered if he would ever feel that aliveness and urgency again the rest of his days. He was wistful for the frontier encounter, the cliff edge. This cliff edge is a frontier where passion, belonging, and need call for our presence, our powers, and our absolute commitment.

To approach work in this manner is not merely to look for constant excitement but to join a conversation with the great cycles of existence, cycles that often terrify us even as they call on the best of us. I think of my sisters, hospital nurses, intimately familiar with the once great, now fallen and achingly vulnerable: the former CEO wandering the hospital corridors in a dreamlike dementia, calling, "John . . . John . . . John"; the track athlete slowly moving his legs after the car smash, his triumph now confined to the slightest increase in their arc of movement. It is astonishing how much of our everyday work has powerful life-or-death consequences: the firefighter on the fragile roof, the policeman on the street, the electrical engineer bringing power back to a darkened neighborhood. The teacher curses his way to school and then says exactly the right thing at the right time to the vulnerable, listening adolescent. All good work should have an edge of life and death to it, if not immediately apparent, then to be found by ardently exploring its greater context. Absent the edge, we drown in numbness.

In Galapagos, I felt the presence of that cliff edge, almost every day and night—particularly in the night, when we navigated the reef-strewn islands without beacons, lights, or electronic instruments. All we had was the faint illumination of a compass and dead reckoning. Meanwhile, my own inner compass was pointing in a direction I didn't want to go. After years of distant biological conceptualization, I was being given a personal introduction to the

800-pound gorilla called nature. Whatever it wanted, in the end, nature seemed to get. The enormous power and reach of the natural world in Galapagos stirred me to search for whatever courage I could muster to face life in a way that was not based at its root on dread.

The closest I had come to this raw power in my own growing had been the fierce moorland winds of my native Yorkshire. As I looked into the wave forms cresting past the boat at night, I remembered the North Country fogs, the winter blizzards, the unending bogs. My mind roved back over the austere beauty of those seas of moss and peat. I couldn't help but think of an equally fierce young woman who lived on the shoreline of those moors.

No coward soul is mine,
No trembler in the world's storm-troubled sphere:
I see Heaven's glories shine,
And faith shines equal, arming me from fear.

That was Emily Brontë, author of *Wuthering Heights,* at her own cliff edge, in defiance of all the fearful dangers standing between her and her work. She had to find a way across a very storm-troubled sphere. She spoke not only of the tearing elemental nature of that North Country wind but also of the forces she fought against in her own lifetime as a writer and a woman; a woman very visible to herself but barely visible to the masculine Victorian world into which she was born. What was the faith that armed her from fear? Fear of the wind and fear of societal displeasure? To my mind, it was some kind of intimate conversation that Emily was able to sustain, along with her sisters, Charlotte and Anne, with the more frightening, often hidden forces of life.

Emily Brontë lived at the cliff edge of life from a very early age. She and her sisters, along with their brother, Branwell, lost their mother as young children. Her father, though present in the house, lived mostly in his study and his church and left them to parent themselves. There were no real adult voices advising imaginative caution. For most of us, an inner parental voice continually keeps the world at bay. It says, "Life is precarious; you young cannot know how precarious. Don't add to the sum total of difficulty that awaits you: Stay off the moors: Stay off the ocean, stay away from the edge, don't follow the intensity of your more passionate dreams, find safe work, and adventure not into your own nature lest it lead you directly into nature itself. Adventure only on the weekends of life and not in the working week."

These wary voices are deep inside us, whispering into our ears on the edge of a decision or as a background chorus as we walk into the office every day, even as we grow into our own middle age. Despite the lineaments of our streamlined organizations, the flow charts and the carefully calculated retirement, when we neglect this more forceful conversation with the edges of existence, a great part of us feels entirely subject to the mercies of the windblown world that has now become a stranger to us.

THE EDGE OF THE UNKNOWN

Stories of near disaster on dangerous shores are not so far, then, from the dynamics that underlie a normal workday. Without the presence of an edge in our lives, much of our work is bent toward keeping chaos at bay, staving off financial disaster, or integrating the differing wave forms of dozens of unpredictable people in a given organization. In the midst of it all, like a child determined to be noticed above the surrounding din, we have to keep up the noisy drumroll of results. Wave against wave, work is an uncharted sea. Any difficult conversation, any sudden change of career, we feel, may lead to a possible shipwreck. Yet increasingly now, despite our wish for safety, there is less that resembles a steady career or a straight career path. This moment of reckoning under the lava cliff speaks to the many dangerous arrivals in a life of work and to the way we must continually forge our identities through our endeavors.

A Necessary Simplicity

Whether it is a place like Galapagos or a place like our office, if we are serious about our work we tend to find ourselves apprenticed to something much larger than we expected, something that calls on more of our essence than we previously imagined, something seemingly raw and overpowering. The young, exhausted lawyer glimpses, late one evening, the enormous commitment needed for her future partnership; the apprentice violin maker can only marvel at the older man's simultaneous ease and absolute precision with the tiny wood plane. Seemingly superhuman forces always call on individual human beings to simplify themselves. A kind of simplification, achieved day by day, hour by hour, in our given work, right into the essence of what needs to be done. That simplified essence can terrify us, as I found in Galapagos. And that simplified essence is not to be found so easily, as T. S. Eliot indicated, using the metaphor of the sea so brilliantly. It seems to be hidden, between the waves themselves, because indeed, newly arrived at the edge, we have not yet developed the faculties that will allow us to see the pattern in full.

Not known, because not looked for
But heard, half heard, in the stillness
Between two waves of the sea.
Quick now, here, now, always—
A condition of complete simplicity
(Costing not less than everything) . . .
              —T. S. ELIOT
            "Four Quartets"

Our drama aboard the *Bronzewing,* adrift beneath the lava cliff, almost cost us everything, but our collective response to the near disaster was anything but simple. I will never forget the pale distress of the captain as he first appeared and looked quickly from the cliff to me. In an instant, everything was said. Under the stricken white parchment of his face, I could see the sense of guilt plainly written for the world. He didn't see it in mine because I was not yet fully aware of my part in the drama and I had hidden my contribution to the disaster at the bottom of a chasm yet to be explored. I could afford to be smug and artificially generous on the surface though secretly hold him to blame, even while my smugness slowly began to unravel from within.

LOOKING INTO THE ABYSS

My first reaction was the easy one. I could see only his neg-lect—his almost criminal neglect, to our seagoing minds—as *captain*. He had slept through not only the anchor dragging but our long, long, nighttime drift. I saw his painful humiliation too, because I, the mere naturalist on board, had discovered our plight. But there was a rising disquiet beginning to beat in my own chest. I and my fellow crew member Carlos, really knew our boat better than this new captain, and we were definitely more familiar with the particular anchorage from which we had drifted. We should have persisted in our shared opinion the previous night about our need to put out a second anchor line. We should have dropped another anchor without consultation, as crews are wont to do when they do not want to argue with their captain. We should have woken too.

No matter that the inherited world of the sea told us that the captain is the be-all and end-all of all responsibility, we had all con-tributed to the lapse, the inexcusable lapse. The edge is no place for apportioning blame. If we had merely touched that cliff, we would have been for the briny deep, crew and passengers alike. The under-tow and the huge waves lacerating against that undercut, barnacle-encrusted fortress would have killed us all.

Nothing was said; Carlos had appeared in the cockpit as we left the shadow of the cliff, knew all instantly, and disappeared just as quickly. We motored away, back toward the anchorage, the sleep-ing passengers blissfully unaware of how close they had been to a sudden, shocked and very violent end. I could hear Carlos starting on the breakfast. Nothing could be said—there was nothing to be said. The near-disaster seemed beyond any post-mortem, but my mind swung back and forth, unable to rest. There was nothing criminal in dragging our single line; we had gone to sleep in a flat calm, with the wind coming up suddenly in the night. Rabida Island has a notorious, difficult, sloping beach, unable to hold an anchor in any kind of blow.

It was the captain's sleeping through it all that had been so shocking. Captains do not sleep when wind or weather changes, they wake up. More secretly Carlos and I were shocked that we had slept on, too, but the captain was there in all his inherited and burdened glory and thus convenient for the blame. Historically, *captaincy* is not just a post, it is an inhabitation, the boat a second skin. It is parenthood, and even in your sleep an invisible monitoring consciousness should wake to the least whimper, to the most minute change in motion, never mind a dragged anchor and a two-mile rocking drift on a rough night sea.

It was all the more disturbing when Carlos and I thought of our previous captain. A robust, strapping man, bred to the sea, Raphael had always been preternaturally alert and omnipresent, appearing on deck at the least sign of trouble. Raphael had been someone in the midst of the main event at all times and out of that example galvanized us to the same pitch of attention. We had made a tight, mutually trusting crew on board the *Bronzewing*. Raphael ran a *very* tight ship, but we also laughed, fished, and dove for lobster together. Raphael had guided my Spanish, and I had taught him the rudiments of English. He was good, very good for my first real apprenticeship to the sea, and then suddenly he was gone, promoted away from us. We had privately mourned Raphael's rise to one of the larger yachts and the breaking up of our little team, though we had said little to one another at the time. Now, it was easy to feel an outer confirmation of our inner sense that there was a stranger in our midst. We were surrounded by the far-stretching, changing ocean every day; trust in one another in the midst of this unknown, ever-shifting immensity was unspoken but incredibly important. The new captain had let us down. No matter that the *Bronzewing* was now forging purposefully back to Rabida Island, we were all in our hearts and minds temporarily adrift.

CAPTAINS COURAGEOUS

The great irony was that in his all-knowing alertness, we had allowed Raphael to lull us subtly into a lack of responsibility at the very core; we were alert as crew members, but Raphael had so filled his role of captain to capacity that we ourselves had become incapacitated in one crucial area: We had given up our own inner sense of captaincy. Somewhere inside us we had come to the decision that ultimate responsibility lay elsewhere. I told this story of near disaster to a recently retired admiral from the U.S. navy. He listened with a lifetime's experience at sea, looked me straight in the eye, and summed it all up: "A good crew doesn't let a new captain fail."

A six-month-old child is admitted to the hospital with early congestive heart failure. The doctor prescribes *Rogoxin* which steadies the heart rate but can be lethal above a certain level. The doctor places the decimal point in the wrong place and prescribes 0.9 mg instead of 0.09. An experienced nurse catches the error and consults with another nurse. They both say it is too high; they take it to a second doctor for a second opinion; he does the recalculation and says the first doctor was right. They give the *Rogoxin* at the higher dose and the child dies. Who had the captaincy? Somewhere inside themselves the nurses thought the doctor was the real captain no matter the outward circumstances and that they were powerless. They were not; they had the captaincy, but not the courage of a captain's convictions.

THE LOST LEADER

Sailing back to our anchorage in the midst of that silence set me to thinking of the edges and boundaries of everyday identity and especially the way that we live at the edges of our identity in work. Beyond the edge we have established for ourselves lies the unknown, where we often feel powerless and ready to blame. Above the throb of the engine, I was desperate to blame someone, crying out for someplace to lodge an ultimate sense of responsibility, and panicking a little because it came to rest nowhere but on my own shoulders. But how we long for that parental image of a captain or leader to carry the burden.

"O Captain! my Captain!"

Walt Whitman cried out to Lincoln, seeing in his president a stabilizing, organizing force, that could guide him, not only through a terrible Civil War, but through the generous, untidy sea of Whitman's own life. Whitman's lines of poetry are generally long, marvelous, out-of-control wave-forms. You see the great outlines of life through the way his poetry crashes and froths on the headlands and reefs of whatever he was attempting to describe. But in Lincoln, Whitman intuited someone who was neither claimed by the chaos of the waves nor chained by the stability of dry land, someone living right at the conversational cliff edge of a whole nation. In the bloody American Civil War, Whitman worked in frontline hospitals tending the wounded and the soon to be dead; he must have seen Lincoln as the great survivor, a man who lived through a whole series of near shipwrecks—in those perilous times, a true captain. Lincoln seemed to be steering the country even as it was convulsed by civil war, guiding a vessel that seemed to be coming apart in the bitterness of slavery. Even in difficulty, the president seemed awake, present, alert to the veering winds of conflict, trimming a way through the elements.

> *"O Captain! my Captain! Our fearful trip is done,*
> *The ship has weathered every rack, the prize we*
> *sought is won,*
> *The port is near, the bells I hear, the people all*
> *exulting . . .*

How desperately we need that captain. Someone to rely on, someone who will awaken when we are asleep, someone to take care of us without making it too obvious, but someone obviously to blame when everything goes wrong. We love a captain in our personal kingdom, our politics, our country, our workplace, and especially in the reflection of our own mirror. All or nothing. I am the captain, or someone else is. *The Boss.* We say, all our resentments held in suspension while the word soaks up our sense of responsibility. In the image of that all-knowing presence is everything we think we need.

Until, that is, Lincoln is suddenly assassinated and we find ourselves immediately orphaned in the world. In the all-powerful presence of a great leader, it is easy to remain unaware of our own personal compass, a direction, a willingness to meet life unmediated by any cushioning parental presence. Whitman's cry for Lincoln is the cry for those selfsame qualities brought to life in the heart of every individual. The shock of Lincoln's death was the shock of living without his outer image, of having to live out that legacy firsthand.

> *What do you see Walt Whitman?*
> *Who are they you salute, and that one after another*
>   *salute you?*
>   —WALT WHITMAN
>   "Salut au Monde!"

The death of anyone close to us is always a form of salutation, a simultaneous good-bye to their physical presence and a deep hello to a more intimate imaginal relationship now beginning to form in their absence. My captain in the outer world had essentially been killed, he had let me down, and I was struggling to salute and recognize a personal sense of captaincy that lived in everyone. It seems emblematic to me also of the times in which we live—when, for many, all of the outer captains have been done away with; by their own actions, by our cynicism, or perhaps more truly because we no longer want captaincy to be static and concentrated in single personalities but movable and available, a provenance of our own.

WAKING THE CAPTAIN

In the moment that I had woken in a panic and seen the captain still asleep in his bunk, simply for the sake of sheer survival I had not had time to wake him and was forced to rouse an equivalent responsibility in myself. It may be that we all come to this threshold at one time or another in our lives when suddenly the person on whom we have conferred captaincy is no longer present or available. It may be their literal absence or a sudden insight in a meeting room that the man or woman at the end of the table cannot be relied on. We look and look and finally realize they are not available, they are deep inside some insulation which cannot be engaged and therefore cannot be trusted. Not because they are bad people but because they are not awake people. At that moment, whatever their outer title, to us they are no longer the captain. At that moment we are orphaned from a familiar parent-child relationship but we are also, if we can rise to the occasion, thankfully emancipated. We are ushered into an adult-adult conversation with our own powers. Something must be done: We must speak out, take the wheel, call the rest of the crew ourselves, or, if all of these avenues are blocked, abandon ship, resign, and go elsewhere.

Whenever we attempt something difficult there is always a sense that we have to wake some giant slumbering inside ourselves, some greater force as yet hidden from us. We look for better work by first looking for a better image of ourselves. We stir this inner giant to life in order to find the strength to live out the life we want for ourselves. We want to live that image not for abstract heroic reasons but because we are desperate for more presence, more responsiveness, more alertness in our work. But first we must be able to recognize the image.

WAKING THE GIANT

What do we look for in the hidden giant, the captain that is living inside us, as yet asleep? The same qualities we admire in good leaders we see in the outside world. What are the qualities that make us love the good captains, the good leaders, the good bosses of this world? What is it about them that brings out the best in us and makes us want to shine not only for them but for something we seem to be discovering simultaneously in ourselves? What is it about a great leader that allows us to be ourselves despite or even because of our faults and difficulties? Why are we so existentially disappointed when someone in a responsible position fails in that responsibility, when the captain fails to be a captain? Is it because, like Whitman, we feel without them we are losing a little of the color and texture of life, that when we lose them we also lose a little faith in our own calling?

One of the outer qualities of great captains, great leaders, great bosses is that they are unutterably themselves. This is what makes their stature so gigantic in our imaginations. They are living at a frontier, a cliff edge, in a kind of exhilaration that we want to touch in our own lives. The best stay true to a conversation that is the sum of their own strange natures and the world they inhabit, and do not attempt to mimic others in order to get on. Though they may try sincerely to communicate with others, these giants will not make themselves *like* everyone else in order to do it. There is no replacing a Mandela, the present Dalai Lama, a Rosa Parks, a Martin Luther King, a Churchill, a Susan B. Anthony, not because there are no more great leaders like them to come but because there are no more of those particular individuals.

Rosa Parks was tired, not heroic when she refused to move to the back of the bus, it was her own tiredness and she stood by it, as if she was reclaiming an edge of exhaustion she hadn't allowed herself to feel until then. It was the tiredness of work but also the utter exhaustion of being invisible, of not being seen. It was as if the true inner reality of her tiredness suddenly became the only thing visible to her, and having touched it, she was damned if she was going to let anyone take even that away from her. She took an element of her nature normally seen in a bad light and by inhabiting it fully turned a form of extreme tiredness that we normally consider as lead, into gold. She was a tiny individual who, because of her intense refusal to be anyone but her tired self, looms in giant fashion over our historical perspective of the sixties.

At the other end of the spectrum, when we come to the image of a classic war leader, I think of Churchill, no bland product of strategizing spin doctors, but a cigar-chomping, brick laying eccentric of the first order. No Puritan either, Churchill did all of his morning work while comfortable in bed and, during a long life, drank his own very substantial weight in Champagne and brandy many times over. He had suffered satire, discouragement, near bankruptcy and political exile, yet when Britain was drifting onto the rocks of defeat in May 1940, he was awake and ready to face the shadows of Nazi Germany. He offered to the British people not the need to please, but " blood, sweat and tears," the will to survive, and a glimmering hope of future triumph. Britain had a giant to wake because Churchill was a giant self, independent of any outer recognition.

I think also, against all my better instincts, of Margaret Thatcher, much loved in the United States but mostly disliked now in the Britain that elected her to power throughout the eighties. Her great triumph was to smash an old complacent political order that was doing no one any good, but to do it in a way which disenfranchised many and set people at each other's throats. That being said, it took a certain species of obnoxious self-righteousness peculiar only to herself to be able to do it. I vividly remember being backstage at an international event in San Francisco with the former Soviet leader Mikhail Gorbachev and former U.S. president George Bush, waiting for the proceedings to begin. All at once, the door seemed to blow open, and from the outer world, Margaret swept in with all the impact on our quiet backwater of a tropical cyclone. In moments she had roiled the calm backstage ambiance and bent everything and everyone to her enormous will.

Firstly, she told the former president of the Soviet empire to sit down and rest because he looked exhausted, then she turned upon the former leader of the free world and told him in no uncertain terms that he looked piqued and must immediately get something from the buffet. George went with the tide and complied. Finally she pinned Bernard Shaw of CNN up against the wall and insisted that he reveal the questions she was to be asked that evening in front of the television cameras. All protestations of journalistic freedom were batted aside and Bernard was worn down and snapped at like a sheepdog with an errant ewe until he surrendered up at least a tiny morsel of information. This done, he was released and allowed to assume an upright position.

I couldn't help but marvel at the sheer bloody-minded willfulness of the woman. No matter my prejudices against her, she was unutterably herself, a force of nature. I thought to myself that there was nothing essentially wrong with her; whatever the negative fallout of her political reign, it was the fault of those of us, her ministers, her political opposition, the voting population, who could not stand up to her and be just as robust in our ability to say *no*. There had been almost no one who had had enough confidence in themselves to meet her on equal terms. When in the presence of that kind of power we give up on our own powers, we allow for a kind of despotism. We allow an individual to be themselves in isolation from all other individuality, which is good for neither the Margaret Thatchers of this world nor the world on which they leave their mark.

To wake the giant inside ourselves, we have to be faithful to our own eccentric nature, and bring it out into conversation with the world. We can rely on the conversation itself to iron out the selfish aspects of our nature. In baseball parlance, we have to step up to the plate; in the parlance of the soul's exploration, we must step to the frontier of the unknown where there are great possibilities at play, where we do not know where our courageous speech might lead us. We have to say *no* just as firmly as we say *yes*. Yes, we want the attributes of leadership but often falter in the presence of the real thing.

Standing Up to Others

We love a strong captain, but how do we live out our own captaincy in the shadow of those who seem to overwhelm our own nursling qualities by the overpowering nature of their character or competency? Is it because we have no equivalent image inside ourselves to match the outer image which is trampling over our world? Margaret Thatcher was famous for her tyrannical hold over her ministers—almost all of them men, almost all of them products of Britain's traditional public schools. They had absolutely no experience of powerful women behaving in this fashion. Perhaps they had read about certain Greek goddesses in their classical studies, but the only woman they would have had any daily contact with through their schooling would have been the matron; the school nurse. They had absolutely no inner image of a wilder, more willful femininity to correspond to this outer political fury, and they were almost all helpless before her. Orbiting her central sun, they became a bland circle of yes-men caught in the grip of her gravitational influence.

In order to stand up against a force of nature, we often have to find that same elemental nature inside ourselves. Many times in our work lives we walk through the office door with our shoulders hunched to our necks, feeling powerless and bullied by those who hold power over us. Our refusal to stand up to those who harass us on a daily basis becomes, in effect, a lack of faith in our own voice, and the nature that that voice bestows on us. A vicious circle begins in which our refusal to speak out confirms our vulnerability and increases our invisibility. We feel certain that we will lose our job, our position, our career, and no one will ever look at us again. Or, like the ministers who surrounded Margaret Thatcher, we may not even know how to begin a conversation with that kind of irrational power. Sometimes we are rightly quiet in the face of dire consequences for our career or our families, but more often than not we are simply living in the shadow of our own fears.

I remember Joel, a consultant friend of mine, telling me of his failure to stand up to one bullying CEO early in his career. Joel recounts with some wonder how he had collapsed completely at a crucial moment of confrontation because there was no inner giant to wake inside him. Quite the contrary, not only did Joel see himself being fired if he stood up to the CEO, but he had the incredible and irrational image of himself living out the rest of his existence as a bag lady on the streets of Berkeley, his then home in California. The prospect of being fired was not irrational to Joel, the image of himself as a bag lady was. What Joel had stumbled into was an unspoken fear which he had not yet explored, and which hid from him the deeper strengths of his own nature. As soon as he found himself in that unspeakable territory, his will collapsed. The fact is that whatever Joel was most afraid of he would surely become if he confronted the angry CEO, no matter that it involved the little imaginative matter of a sex change. Joel was sure that the CEO would talk to every other CEO in his native California and bar him from a fruitful career. But Joel went on to say that whatever courage he had learned now as a consultant in his organizational work came from that moment. Joel realized that in order to be effective he had to take an inventory of his own fears; whatever he did not know of his own fears would blind him at the moments when he was faced with an unknown. Joel made a further crucial distinction: He did not have to overcome his fears, he simply had to know *what* he was afraid of.

Almost always when we ask hard questions about leaders and leadership, we have to ask hard questions of ourselves, too. We have to take an inventory not only of the gifts we have to give but of the gifts we are afraid of receiving. What are we afraid of, what stops us from speaking out and claiming the life we want for ourselves? Quite often it is a sudden horrific understanding of the intimate and extremely personal nature of the exploration. When we ask in a serious manner for those marvellous outer abstracts of courage, captaincy, and greatness, we set in motion an exploration that tests us to the very core. We suddenly realize the intensely personal nature of all these attributes. Stephen Spender has it very well in his poem, The Truly Great.

> *I think continually of those who were truly great*
> *Who, from the womb, remembered the soul's history*
> *Through corridors of light, where the hours are suns,*
> *Endless and singing. Whose lovely ambition*
> *Was that their lips, still touched with fire,*
> *Should tell of the spirit, clothed from head to foot in song.*
> *And who hoarded from the Spring branches*
> *The desires falling across their bodies like blossoms.*
>
> *What is precious is never to forget*
> *The essential delight of the blood drawn from ageless springs*
> *Breaking through rocks in worlds before our earth.*
> *Never to deny its pleasure in the morning's simple light,*
> *Nor its grave evening demand for love;*
> *Never to allow gradually the traffic to smother*
> *With noise and fog the flowering of the spirit.*

Near the snow, near the sun, in the highest fields
See how these names are feted by the waving grass,
And by the streamers of white cloud,
And whispers of wind in the listening sky.
The names of those who in their lives fought for life,
Who wore at their hearts the fire's center.
Born of the sun, they travelled a short while toward the sun,
And left the vivid air signed with their honour.

—STEPHEN SPENDER

Spender talks of hoarding from the spring branches the desires falling across our bodies like blossoms. A simultaneous harvest and fading away, growth and disappearance, that involves an exploration of both sides of life's equation, our continual appearance and disappearance as if rehearsing for the ultimate disappearance in death. Is there any other real source of courage? At the end is left only a vivid signature in the air, an echo of Keats's epitaph, "Here lies one whose name was writ in water." Not a testament to loss but a courageous acceptance that we make our mark and then move on, but it is the making that makes the meaning.

PERSONALITY AND PASSION

The great question about leadership, about taking real steps on the pilgrim's path, is the great question of any individual life: how to make everything more personal. How to understand life or leadership not as an abstract path involving devious strategies but more like an inhabitation, a *way* of life, a conversation, a captaincy; an expression of individual nature and gifts and a familiarity with the specific nature of your own desires and fears. In a conversation there is always more than one voice, and one of the voices must be our own or it is no conversation at all. We do not try to overpower others at work with our voice in order to have a conversation, nor do we substitute someone else's for our own, but we are there, we are present, we are heard. We play the tension like a violin string at concert pitch. We stop looking for heroes to come and show us the path to glory, but we do not ignore the courageous example of others. In their presence, or under the influence of their reputation, we attempt to find the same inner correspondences in our own bodies that will allow us to take the next courageous step that we can also call our own.

In order to assume our captaincy, we should not genuflect before the imposing array of other captains. We must stop indulging in worshipful idolatry of Bill Gates or Jack Welch (in their wiser moments, they surely wish to escape from that idolatry), and put our energies toward taking the short but difficult next step on our own pilgrim's path to self-knowledge. So long as this path is a real conversation with the greater world, it will lead us right to the frontier of presence we desire. Taking any step that is courageous, however small, is a way of bringing any gifts we have to a surface, where they can be received. For that we have to come out of hiding, out from behind the insulation. In a way, we come to an understanding of ourselves in our work according to where we have established our edge. Wherever our edge of understanding has been established is the very place we should look more intently, but it is also the very place that fills us most with fear. In my own captain's failure I had come to an edge that I had previously refused.

COMING OUT OF HIDING: BEING THE CAPTAIN

After our near disaster beneath the cliff face, how did I see the captain's failure? It had everything to do with being in hiding. Somehow this new captain, whose professional world was made up of his maritime experience, the boat, its itinerary, its crew, its passengers and the wild elements that surrounded it, had allowed his attention to retreat into an insulated room inside himself that had no connection with the immediacy of his outer world. In the rough territory of the Galapagos, washed by the restless Pacific, the result was a neglect and forgetfulness, a sleep in which others could die.

There is a marvelous relationship between the living body of a sailing vessel and the actual human body we try to inhabit every day in the workplace. Our attempt to convey an idea to others in the office, or our attempt to show others that we are useful and have something to give, is a way of feeling physically present in the world. Our bodies and our personalities are vessels, and leadership, like captaincy, is a full inhabitation of the vessel. Having the powerful characteristics of captaincy or leadership of any form is almost always an outward sign of a person inhabiting their physical body and the deeper elements of their own nature. In the same way, to sleep through crucial moments of our work life is to eventually find ourselves on the rocks, to put ourselves or our organizations in danger.

It is not that a captain cannot sleep, but even in sleep theirs should be a cultivated attentiveness, which is essential at sea. It is something akin to the way we can wake ourselves at a specific time for an important occasion even if we have forgotten to set the bedside alarm, except this is a continuous alertness—accessible even in the deepest modes of sleep. Every turn of the tide or the weather is important. A good captain wakes as soon as the wind veers or the rhythm of the waves lapping at the hull increases.

Waking in response to change is, in effect a litmus test of identity for a leader or a captain, because the ability to know even in unconscious modes what is occurring at the surface speaks to the way that the attributes of seamanship have soaked right through to the core of the captain's identity. Even when a captain rests, he or she does it in conversation with the rhythm of the ocean. The life of the edge is perceived right through to the interior, even in darkness, even in sleep. At sea, this edge is the skin of the boat and the way that edge responds to the living commands of the ocean and the moving air. This edge is more often than not represented by all the courageous conversations we must continually have to keep in touch with the dynamics affecting work; by staying aware of this elemental edge, we can more readily keep to the bearing indicated by our inner compass.

Once we begin to engage those elemental edges through daily courageous speech, we start to build a living picture of our own nature, exactly the same way a captain gets to know her vessel and the particular way it reacts to the elements that surround it. As captain of our soul's journey, we feel the angle of the sails, the creak and strain of the ropes, the lean of the tiller, and learn the particular hum and song of our conversation with the elements. It is this conversation that gives us not only our powers of survival but a music of exhilaration for our journey and arrival.

It seems to me that every human life has the elements of a sea voyage, of a journey and an arrival. That every human life is also like a vessel that contains innumerable other lives for which we have a deep responsibility. That this vessel journeys from one unknown sea to another as we go through important epochs of our lives, and that every soul's journey in the world is like a captaincy—that is, an identity which is necessarily attentive, powerful, and responsible, but not fixed, more like a meeting place of the elements in which the known vessel and the unknown sea must join in vital conversation. Out of this conversation we create a directional movement in the world that not only ensures our survival but creates exhilaration, the wind on our face, an immersion in the present whilst we simultaneously experience the joy of speeding toward our destination.

To my mind, this captaincy, this responsible and responsive presence, this creation of an elemental meeting place inside oneself or in one's organization or society, is not just an individual dynamic, but one in which the whole of humanity is collectively engaged. We are living at a time when much of the way we see and describe ourselves is under immense strain from the currents of change that swirl around us. Our old fixed, terrestrial ideas and the language to describe those ideas do not seem terribly well adapted to the fluidity of our new ocean world. We are each being impacted in enormous, far-reaching ways by the tides of ecological and technological change and the sudden realization that we inhabit a much more complex, intimate universe than we imagined. We intuit that we are about to cross a great expanse to a new place, but our maritime abilities, our sense of captaincy, our courage, our responsiveness— individually and collectively—are under severe test.

IMAGINATION AMID COMPLEXITY

The severest test of work today is not of our strategies but of our imaginations and identities. For a human being, finding good work and doing good work is one of the ultimate ways of making a break for freedom. In order to find that freedom in the midst of the complex world of work, we need to cultivate simpler, more ele- mental identities truer to the template of our own natures. We must understand that we carry enough burdens in the outer world not to want to replicate that same sense of burden in our inner selves. We need a sense of spaciousness and freedom, but find we can claim that freedom only by living out a radical, courageous simplicity—a simplicity based on the particular way we belong to the world we inhabit. If we ignore our simpler necessities, the attempt to create a complex professional identity most often buries us in layers of insu- lation through which it is impossible to touch our best gifts. Our lives take the form of absence. Like the captain asleep below, we become exhausted from the effort needed to sustain our waking identities. The day may be full, we may be incredibly busy, but we have forgotten who is busy and why we are busy. We lose the con- versation, we lose our calling, we lose our sense of captaincy. To wake up and assume the captaincy no matter the perceived outer hierarchy, we have to realize that our lives are at stake; the one unique life, entirely our own, it is possible for each of us to live.

Death is much closer to each of us then we will admit; we must not postpone that living as if we will last forever.

We speak of genius when we speak of leadership, hoping for some of that elusive genius in ourselves, but the word *genius* in its Latin originality means simply, *the spirit of a place*. The genius of Galapagos lies in its being unutterably itself; the genius of an individual lies in the inhabitation of their peculiar and particular spirit in conversation with the world. Genius is something that is itself and no other thing.

The task is simple and takes a life pilgrimage to attain, to inhabit our life fully, just as we find it, and in that inhabitation, let everything ripen to the next stage of the conversation. We do this because that is how we make meaning and how we make everything real. The core act of leadership must be the act of making conversations real. The conversations of captaincy and leadership are the conversations that forge real relationships between the inside of a human being and their outer world, or between an organization and the world it serves. All around these conversations, the world is still proceeding according to mercies other than our own. This is the ultimate context to our work. The cliff edge of mortality is very near. We must know how easy it is to forget, how easy it is to drift onto the rocks and put our lives to hazard. Everything is at stake, and everything in creation, if we are listening, is in conversation with us to tell us so.

IV

A Star for Navigation:

Ambition, Horizon, and Arrival

The bell clanged behind the cabin door and with one last hungry look toward the horizon, the passengers and crew went below for the waiting meal. One brave soul who wished to remain on deck was bullied back into the cabin by the imploring, anguished, Spanish of the cook, and vanished at last through the door. I stayed where I was. I didn't have a choice; I was on watch, but it didn't matter. I was hungry but very glad to be left alone at the wheel. This wind was no ordinary wind, and the fiery sky behind me was no ordinary sunset. It was no sunset at all. The sky was red because it was literally on fire, plumed and clouded by an erupting volcano filling the western sky. The strength of the wind came from the heat of the eruption lifting great draughts of air into the upper atmosphere and stirring the still surface air below to life. We were in a veritable Mistral of wind, a powerful but steady force blowing toward the volcano, replacing the lifting air being drawn toward the fiery summit.

Once alone, I was able to enter a joy that goes beyond the

bounds of any happiness you can show in company. At the same time, as if to push my good spirits over the edge, a crowd of dolphins came leaping southward toward our bow, their fins curving and disappearing. I looked back at the glowing, late afternoon sky and then forward at the taut mass of sail, and exulted at the sheer beauty of the islands that had become my home. I looked at everything as if I might never see it again. This was my last tour. I was leaving Galapagos at last and moving on—moving on to do what, I did not know. Beneath the surface incandescence I had the profound regret of leaving a place that had given me everything I had desired in a work and a life. Everything in the previous decade of my young life from the age of thirteen had been bent toward my arrival in a work or a place like Galapagos, and now I had set myself to travel beyond that horizon into uncharted seas. I felt both vulnerable and emboldened at the same time.

There is a strange way in which at each crucial juncture in our work lives, whenever we leave the familiar behind, we become in a certain way, childlike again. In our vulnerability we look for the grown-up equivalent of parental help, but we are also thrown back upon those images and inner resources that are the province of the dreaming youngster. The divorced woman sits in her empty house recalling the young woman who first entered it in marriage. The retiring professor recalls his first enthusiastic discoveries in the subject he has read for a lifetime. The jobless manager begins in her grief to familiarize herself with possibilities at the very center of feeling unwanted. The single most useful power inside us at these critical times is the expressive imagination, that part of us that dreams and creates images representative of both our deepest desires and the way we feel we are made for a continuing work in the world. The part of us staring hard at the horizon for celestial clues as to our relative position on the moving sea we call a life.

First Horizons

Every work begins as an intimation and discovery. Like the first time as a child we walk to the edge of a Yorkshire field, glimpse a new horizon, and immediately want to go there. We do not know where the horizon will take us. We have a glimmering, an inclination, a notion that somehow we will find something beyond our present knowledge. The excitement is palpable and belongs to the horizon and our young anticipatory bodies at the same time. We run toward it, glad and unthinking, the mere presence of horizon itself grants us a sense of freedom. This sense of freedom is not confined to physical landscape. I remember the absolute sense of excitement at nine years old, when I picked up my first book of poetry and read it as if I had discovered a secret code to my future life—which, as it turned out, I had. In it I glimpsed an imaginative, literate horizon which was worth taking a lifetime to reach. I had the same experience at twelve years old when I first saw Jacques Cousteau on our tiny black-and-white television screen and conceived the strange notion of studying marine biology. To my young mind, the small, rounded square of the television set on which he and his ship *Calypso* appeared, represented an unaccountable vastness; it gave me a feeling that there was work in the world that could sail you off the small screen of your present life into something astonishing and indescribable, a world inhabited by creatures and tidal forces unfamiliar and deliciously wild. It was life as horizon and excitement.

Each of us, somewhere in the biography of our childhood, remembers a moment where we felt a portion of the world calling and beckoning to us. We are creatures of belonging, and as our growing consciousness as a child forms we look for the expressions of our belonging in every quarter. Out of this sense of belonging, the world seems to call to us, to recognize us, and to speak to us directly, the voice itself an embodiment of our particular nature and the way that nature finds a home in the world. At best, this conversation between ourselves and the world *becomes* our work. Sometimes we are able to remember and follow the flow of this conversation, but sometimes as a child we were made to feel powerless by the enclosing adult world, and were bullied into forgetting the horizon it represented. Later, in the middle of the road of our adult lives, in a state of utter forgetfulness, we may wake like Dante, in a dark wood, looking for some inner compass bearing that will steer us to the freedom of that horizon again. The inner compass almost always leads us back toward that childhood we have spent so much time trying to leave behind. We return there not to become a child again but to remember those instinctual joys which filled our imaginations and growing bodies and set our enthusiastic course into the world. There is something trustable about the original enthusiasms of the very young that point directly toward the way we are made.

The poet Wordsworth is probably the most famous investigator of this phenomenon. At twenty-eight, snowbound in the winter of 1798–1799, in a small and unwelcoming German hill town with his sister, Dorothy, Wordsworth felt as far from his work and vocation as he ever would: lost, directionless, bereft of inspiration, all of his previous youthful enthusiasm burned down to nothing. In that frozen winter they had for company only their landlady, a French priest, and a deaf neighbor with bad teeth. He later lamented to a friend about the awfulness of the situation: "With bad German, bad English, bad French, bad hearing and bad utterance you will imagine we have had very pretty dialogues." In the midst of this chilly, inarticulate exile, with the direct emotional help of his sister, he began to call on the only resource available to him: his own physical memories of what it had meant as a child to grow amid the mountains and lakes of his native Cumbria.

He began with the memory of himself as a five-year-old child by the river Derwent: "A naked savage, in the thunder shower." Then, as Stephen Gill says in his biography of the poet,

> Wordsworth releases memories of birds nesting among the perilous crags, of snaring woodcocks in the moonlight, of hooting to the owls across Windemere, and of stealing a rowing boat on Ullswater. The tone of the verse is awed, reverent, above all grateful for the process by which a ten-year-old could hold

> > *unconscious intercourse*
> *With eternal beauty drinking in*
> *A pure organic pleasure from the lines*
> *Of curling mist, or from the smooth expanse*
> *Of waters coloured by the cloudless moon.*

Through the physical aliveness of deep memory, Wordsworth not only kept faith with his newly forming identity as a poet but, by winter's end, had composed 400 lines of blank verse. Lines which were to form the core of his adult poetic voice and the basis of his greatest work, *The Prelude*.

ENERGY AND MEMORY

In the small library dedicated to his work in Grasmere, I have actually held the surviving manuscript paper on which Wordsworth rapidly began to form *The Prelude*. It is redolent with discovery and excitement, verses crammed at all angles, in pen, pencil; long rows of words springing out of the ground of his memory. Looking at it, you see not only a personal breakthrough taking place, but the first shaping of our own contemporary appreciation of the natural world. There could be no Environmental Protection Agency, no Sierra Club, no Discovery Channel, no National Parks without the Wordsworths of this world who first began to move our lips again in reverence to and participation with the natural order. In Wordsworth's verses we are taught to see creation once again as a place to grow in, a place indicative of other worlds parallel to ours which necessarily put any single work we do as human beings into smaller and saner perspectives.

Wordsworth's absolute faith in physical memory and the energies they represent is a testament to the way a deeply personal experience, given a work and a vessel to carry it, can speak to thousands of others and affect, in pivotal ways whole worlds and ways of thinking yet to be born. This is one of the great beauties of a private work made manifest in a very public world. Wordsworth, unknown to us, is in every conversation we have about the beauty of a mountain, a seascape, or a sky. Work at its best is the arrival in an outer form of something intensely inner and personal; and the act of working itself—a bridge between the public and the private, a bridge of experience which can be an agony and an ecstasy to cross.

THE INNER TEMPLATE
OF BELONGING

To a child, the world is a beckoning horizon, and as Wordsworth said, *The Child is father of the Man* (and we might add today *mother of the Woman*). Whatever particular horizons drew us as a child are the original patterns and templates of our adult belonging. They are clues as to how we find our measure of happiness and satisfaction in the world. My own nephew, despite his parents' hopes for academic accomplishment, worships his uncle Michael's ability to fix, clean, and set to right anything metallic or mechanical. One day he looked up from his schoolbooks at his mother and said in dreamy fashion, "I just want to be driving around with my uncle Michael, with a big load of washing machines in the back." His mother suddenly knew her son as she had not before. His way in the world is already marked: He may become a mechanic or he may not, but whatever work he does, if he wants any measure of happiness, it will have to hold the qualities of the practical world of which he now dreams. It will have to do with the way things fit together, one to another, or the flow and satisfaction of physical things working right, or put right. Metals and wood, rubber and plastic, these are the objects of his love; already he is beginning, at twelve years old, to build household furniture in his parents' garage. The template of his childhood belonging is there for him to create his adult work. I have witnessed the same love of flight and things that fly at the Boeing company—affections that began in many an engineer's mind at a very young age. To betray these childhood intuitions is to betray our adult participation in a world which has been formed from the clay of those early experiences and recognitions.

But what if we have forgotten? Or find our original dreams and memories painful compared to our present life, and therefore too difficult to bring to mind?

Wordsworth again.

Our birth is but a sleep and a forgetting:
The Soul that rises with us, our life's Star,
Hath had else where its setting,
And cometh from afar:
Not in entire forgetfulness,
And not in utter nakedness,
But trailing clouds of glory do we come
From God, who is our home:
Heaven lies about us in our infancy!
Shades of the prison-house begin to close
Upon the growing Boy,
But He beholds the light, and whence it flows,
He sees it in his joy;
The Youth, who daily farther from the east
Must travel, still is Nature's Priest,
And by the vision splendid,

> *Is on his way attended;*
> *At length the Man perceives it die away,*
> *And fade into the light of common day.*
> —"Intimations of Immortality from
> Recollections of Early Childhood"

The poem is beautifully titled. *Intimations of Immortality*. Not one of us, despite millennia of theological investigation, really knows where we come from or where we go. We especially do not know how our daily work actually fits into that perspective, but most of us have *intimations* of some greater continuum of which we are a part. The intuition is a lifeline to a greater participation beyond our present work, beyond our present horizon. Without it our work finds no greater context. Remembering this life's journey beyond our present daily commute is one of life's great disciplines, but keeping it as a constant, inspiring companion is beyond most of our powers. Sooner or later we forget, we lose sight, we come to a place in our lives where *the vision splendid* begins to fade into the light of common day.

Every person comes to a place, at one time or another in their maturation, of complete loss and deadness, a stark and frightening absence of creativity and enthusiasm, where life seems to retreat away from us like a tide. Our desperate grasping after the outgoing energy only marks our desperation more fully. The old magic seems to be ours no longer, and we look enviously at those still able to create it. This is the very point where deep physical memories are our lifeline to any future we want for ourselves. In effect, somewhere inside us, the child is still running enthusiastically toward a horizon it once glimpsed. Our future life depends on finding this original directional movement in our lives, no matter how far we feel we are into middle age. It calls for a reinvestigation of the way we physically inhabit the world.

SAVING OURSELVES
FROM MIDDLE AND MUDDLE

The interesting thing about the crisis we often associate with middle age is that it is not confined to our lives after forty-five. A lost teenager can exhibit the same sense of drift, the same dark depression, and the same feeling of being walled off behind glass as any graying fifty-year-old. Just like the body of a man or woman encountering middle age, the teenager's new body can also seem a new and uncontrollable force. Middle age is a cyclical visitation throughout our existence. We can experience an early middle-age crisis when we are in the midst of a project that needs desperately to be redefined or redrawn, or we can find middle age when we are only three months into a marriage, as trapped and desperate as if we had been there for thirty years. We can find it staring out of a palatial hotel room when we don't know why we are there or why the company is paying the outrageous bill. Any experience where the tide seems to have left us stranded is a good equivalent. The essence of midlife crisis is that something has to change but the person feels he no longer has the body, the will, or the energy to do it anymore. We look desperately for other bodies. Literally or figuratively.

LOOKING IN THE MIRROR

In the luxurious restaurant, the expensively attired man in his late sixties looks sideways from the table and captures a glimpse in the mirrored wall of himself and his young companion haloed by candlelight. When he first looked he had a smile on his face, but now he is shocked to see what others must see: a beautiful, poised young woman in her twenties sitting with a very, very old man. Her smooth complexion a pale glowing expanse leaning close to the lined territory of his own. When she rises to go to the washroom, he looks again at himself in the mirror, smiles wryly, and admits he is making a fool of himself. When she returns, he has already consigned his amorous ambitions to that capacious place where all our other strange notions go. For her part, she cannot understand why he suddenly seems to have lost interest. "Thank God I was given that glimpse of us both in the mirror," he confided late one night to a friend. "I didn't like what I could see."

Sometimes the body we want is metal and gleaming chrome. One Sunday afternoon sipping coffee in London, I looked into *The Times* newspaper and saw a classified advertisement for a magnificent BMW 750cc. "Driven for only six weeks through midlife crisis," said the tongue-in-cheek description. Of course, no expense is too much for the middle-aged psyche in its external search for youth, and a BMW 750 is the least of it as far as looking for our lost external bodies. We have to marvel that it took the man only six short weeks to find that the glamorous mechanical body was not his own. The glorious roaring machine only a stepping-stone to a kind of deep, throaty energy the owner wanted in his own voice.

There is another side to this: the fact that our sense of success in life can imprison us as much as our sense of failure. We will often fight and starve a little for our work when we begin a given path. Our first courageous steps steel us for robust shocks to our system and help keep us on a steady course toward the life and work we want. But once we are successful, the forces that challenge and assail our integrity are far more subtle. There is nothing to rob the human spirit like the rewards of an upper-middle-class existence. The lawn, the financial commitments, the blurred pages of the up-market catalogues slowly convince us that life is actually our appearance and that any desire, large or small, can be obtained through a toll-free number.

PRETENDING TO BE ALIVE

We may do the same work and do it well, but we may do it well in a way that does not engage our deeper powers in any real conversation, so that we lose any sense of personal edge. We may be admired in our work, but the admiration blinds and insulates us from the loss of something robust and lifelike inside us. We are impersonating, but the impersonation is incredibly subtle because we are, in effect, impersonating ourselves. The surface life is a simulacrum of something we intuit inside ourselves but have not yet really brought to life from the depths. All the while we are slowly in retreat from our own frontier. We create a business around our success, and then the business and busyness of the outer world becomes a world unto itself. Late one night, we find ourselves going over our net worth in black ink again and again to make sure it is real, still there, still earning the same interest. We need the reassurance that we can define a success at least somewhere in our lives; but the repeated lines of scribbled figures on the legal pad are a sure diagnostic feature that our identity is merging more and more with our bank account. If the nest egg were to disappear, we fret that we might disappear, too.

In the decision to leave Galapagos, I was grappling with a midlife crisis come early. Not that I had much in the way of insulating riches—my net worth was not in monetary terms. I had plenty of daily spending money but I had no savings. In that regard I was poor as a church mouse. My fixation was on the glamour of my life in the islands, different but equally obsessive. Where else could you wake to the sound of a fountaining whale's breath through the wood skin of the boat, dive with seals and sharks, and generally live the bronzed life of intrepid adventurer with no bills, no taxes, no mortgage, and all meals and wine found and provided?

I thought of staying on, of course. It was hard to change a work that offered so much for a future work which was only just beginning to glimmer in my imagination. We all thought of staying on—a few guides actually did. But most of us knew we were in a kind of sweet, paradisiacal prison. A naturalist was not very well paid, but that might not have mattered if it had been possible to build the life into anything larger or more satisfying than continually leading small groups of international visitors through the islands. More important, the traveling, moving life of a sailing naturalist guide could not sustain any long-term relationships or any decent private life. It was a work that ripened my powers of attention to creation but stifled the integration of those powers into a mature life I could call my own.

Not only that, but Galapagos had triggered deep memories of other horizons toward which I had run as a child: the horizon of poets and poetry I had loved since I first could read. After my excursion into science, I was beginning to turn again to that memory. I needed it especially to live on the frontier to which the islands had brought me. In Galapagos, I had begun to form a philosophy of existence that demanded a larger language than the scientific one I had concentrated on for the last few years. Scientific language, ironically enough, was not precise enough to describe my experience in those islands. In silent companionship with the life of the Galapagos, I had come to the conclusion that our personal identity, which we think is based upon our beliefs and opinions, is actually more of a function of our ability to pay attention to the world around us. If we had very little in the way of attention for the world, then we actually had little in the way of real existence. The deeper we could look into all those phenomena which seemed to be other than ourselves, the more a discreet identity we could call a self seemed to appear on life's radar screen. Somewhere out there beyond the islands was another work and another life that would support those farther explorations.

It was time to go, to take stock of what we had learned in this work and hold the unique experience like a second childhood memory, another horizon to take us out into the world no matter how unwelcoming that world might seem. We knew that we had the place—like the salt seawater and the local parasites—in our blood, and we would take it with us long after the wheels had lifted from the tarmac of Baltra airport. Though what we would do after this sojourn in paradise, none of us knew. We had these sunlit hours, but after this, the imagination entered darkness. "What do we do after leaving Shangri La?" we guides would ask one another in the bars of Puerta Ayora, laughing and, an instant later, silent and deadly serious.

It seems to me that this question waits in the shadow of every successful life. A koan question for advanced Zen students is "How do you proceed from the top of a hundred-foot pole?" Once you reach a certain stage of mastery, the dangers increase exponentially. In any occupation where we have achieved a degree of competence, we imperceptibly begin to see ourselves as God's gift to whatever world we have decided to occupy with our working bodies.

Every path, no matter how diligently we follow it, can lead to staleness and ennui. We might reach dizzying heights in our organization, occupy the top floor of any given building, or, as a zoologist, make it to the Galapagos islands, but if we lose our horizon and the excitement of that horizon, our high office or our storied islands can seem like a gilded cage.

WALLS

Ah why did I not pay attention when they were building the
   walls.
But I never heard any noise or sound of builders.
Imperceptibly they shut me from the outside world.
                                    —CONSTANTINE P. CAVAFY
                          "Walls." Translated by Rae Dalven

Sometimes we have built the walls ourselves, but often it is simply the nature of things that walls that once served and sheltered us at certain periods of our life only imprison us when we have remained within their confines for too long. A work emboldens us for a while, and then, if we do not invigorate and reimagine our participation, it begins to enclose us and slowly starve our spirit. Good work done in the same way for too long, or done in the wrong way for any amount of time, eats away our sense of being right with the world.

Often, in order to stay alive, we have to *unmake* a living in order to get back to *living* the life we wanted for ourselves. It is this cycle of making, disintegration, and remaking that is the hallmark of meaningful and creative work. I think of singers like Bob Dylan or Van Morrison, shifting and reinventing themselves album after album. Yeats as a young poet in love with longing and journey, then, in his fierce maturity, writing about the difficulties of arrival. Picasso in his blue period, depicting simple human figures, poignant, marvelous paintings anyone would be glad to have done as the apex of their art, but all flowering into new season through his Cubist vision: eyes and limbs sprouting into a rich summer complexity. The canvas no longer a single dimension but cramming every angle at once into the enriched eye of the beholder.

KEEPING A STAR IN SIGHT

The mainsail on the *Encantada* was huge. It took the entire crew and a little help from any willing passengers to heave it up, and it took a very stiff breeze to warrant heaving it anywhere but into a tight roll on the boom, which is where it almost always stayed. But now, half the sky was filled with this vast red sail, and in front of it, the two foresails were straining to hold the steady wind. Under this spread of canvas, the *Encantada* responded like a wakeful, living thing. I could feel the whole length of the ship alive in the wheel beneath my hands, alert to the least degree of movement. The *Encantada* had been brought to full life, and I felt exactly the same way. Looking back over the last eighteen months, I felt as if these islands had brought *me* to life, had filled my sails, and were bowling me on my way through the waves.

Around me, the sky was beginning to darken, intensifying the red glow of the volcano reflected in our wake, but in the sliver of clear sky to which the bow was pointed, I could see the first stars beginning to appear above the dark blue horizon. I realized that I was pointing the *Encantada* toward home and, emboldened by the elements around me, felt that even though I had not the least idea where that new home would be, there was some equivalent star in the heavens to make that navigation. I thought of the old Latin root of the word *desire,* meaning *de sider, of the stars*. To have a desire in life literally means to keep your star in sight, to follow a glimmer, a bea-con, a disappearing will-o'-the-wisp over the horizon into some-place you cannot yet fully imagine. A deeply held desire is a star that is particularly our own; it might disappear for a while, but when the skies clear we catch sight of it again and recognize the glimmer.

In our youth, we set off running toward our work like the child seeing that new horizon across the fields. In my case, inspired by Cousteau, we might begin to ask our ourselves what we need to do to study marine zoology. At the beginning we run toward it, but we find very quickly that the entire journey demands a more meas-ured pace, and a perseverance we can only learn in the pilgrimage itself. When this night of difficulty falls, we look for a star to hold us to our darkened course. I had no idea of the long hours of species identification ahead of me, the midnight wrestling with the bio-chemical mysteries of the Krebs cycle, the cathedral hush of the examination halls at Bangor University, the trying interview process for the job as a naturalist guide. I often think that if we really knew what territory lay ahead of us and what we might have to put ourselves through to achieve the work we desire, we would probably lock ourselves in a padded room and refuse to emerge. The presence of the star does not excuse us from the difficult territory through which it is guiding us. It hadn't been long before I realized that in order to follow marine biology I had to drop all my beloved art subjects in high school and put myself into the deep salt mines of biology, chemistry, and physics. The path was hard, but the horizon and the star above it must have been real to me, and I did reach it eventually. This day under the volcano on the fiery stern of the *Encantada,* I had finally reached that distant horizon to which I had been aiming. Everything I had wanted in those tiny images on our television set had come true for me. In the vitality of this last voyage through the islands, I could see the unique, almost unspeakable nature of my time in Galapagos: a frontier brush with the natural world that was unfathomable, indescribable, and unrepeatable.

After a year navigating under those tropical skies I found the old human intuition of a star in the heavens whose journey is a template of our own individual path on earth, quite believable. Some nights alone on watch, when the horizon between the phosphorescent sea and the night sky had merged, I felt as if, with a slight nudge of the rudder, the *Encantada* could simply carry on, like an image from a child's book, into the infinity of stars ahead. But exactly because of this experience of arrival, my ambition had finally withered in the actual experience of achieving my goal. Surrounded by the otherworldly miracle of Galapagos, which was actually the real world in too concentrated a form for the human frame to stand, ambition had come to feel less liberating, more confining, bereft of revelation, more like an artificial light I had shone across the water myself; you could direct the beam of ambition to help you see the immediate territory ahead but it would ultimately only illuminate things that were already known to you, and its glare would just as likely rob you of your peripheral night vision. Ambition kills our sense of the miraculous; ambition, ironically, could hide the stars.

Ambition also lacked surprise, it lacked a sense of belonging to the territory through which we travel, and it lacked a sense of the greater story of which we are a part. It lacked completely the understanding that no matter the self-conceited importance of our work, at the end of our lives we are compost for worlds we cannot yet imagine. Ambition takes us toward a horizon but not over it— that line would always recede before our reaching hands. But *desire* is a conversation between our physical bodies, our work, our imaginations, and new worlds that *is* the territory we seek. Ambition takes willpower and constant applications of energy to stay on a perceived bearing; *desire* demands only a constant attention to the unknown gravitational field which surrounds us and from which we can recharge ourselves every moment, as if breathing from the atmosphere of possibility itself. A life's work is not a series of stepping-stones onto which we calmly place our feet, but more like an ocean crossing where there is no path, only a heading, a direction, which, of itself, is in conversation with the elements. Looking back for a sense of reference, we see the wake we have left as only a brief, glimmering trace on the waters.

Years later, I recalled on that exuberant evening like a wake in my memory, the young man in the breeze under the clouded volcano, standing by the wheel that evening on his last voyage through the islands, pointing the *Encantada* toward a low, clear horizon of stars, and wrote this for him.

But still, on the ocean, there is
no path

only the needle's trembling dance
north

. . . followed
without fear,

though the dance now is fear
and calmness
in one movement

seeing

as you look
not only the angry sea
of what you
have denied

but
here,
near at hand,
in the center
of your body,

the rose-fire
of the compass
blossoming
with direction.

V

Out of Ireland:

When does one ever know a human being? Perhaps only after one has realized the impossibility of knowledge and renounced the desire for it and finally ceased to feel even the need of it. But then what one achieves is no longer knowledge, it is simply a kind of co-existence; and this too is one of the guises of love.

—IRIS MURDOCH
Under the Net

The young woman put her head into her hands and looked over the railing of the ferry, watching the gray horizons of Ireland fading to a long, drawn, pencil line on the sea. Now that she was over the first excitement of getting to Dublin and onto the boat, she was thinking back three years, to the real beginning of this journey and the night when her world had changed forever. *Surely,* she said to herself, *she could never have left if I hadn't lost her; if she hadn't gone and left me, gone off into that darkness and left us all to fend for ourselves.* The realization intensified the cold sea wind and the taste of salt spray more sharply, and she pulled the collar of her coat together and looked into the wind. She looked out from the ship's rail above the angry surface of the water and felt the competing tides inside her, the loss of home tugging her to go back, the sheer aloneness of it all, and over it, the exhilaration of leave-taking carrying her on, flooding through her sadness, pulling her over the sea to find good work, to England.

She remembered how everything on that night had started in such a warm and loving way. She had been twelve years old, dressed at last and steeled to go out the door despite her misgivings. She went to her mother's bedside in the dim, evening light. She didn't want to go out to the hall, she didn't feel she had a breath of a song inside her, but her mother wanted her to, and wanted her to sing. She held her mother's hand and told her she didn't want to leave her, she wanted to stay by her side, talking to her at the bedside. As the memories flooded through her, she looked down at the gray surging waves combing into whiteness. She hadn't wanted to go, but her mother had insisted that she dress and go and sing. Her mother had told her, as she stretched up to kiss her, that she had the loveliest voice in Waterford City, that her daughter would carry the competition and there would be none to match her.

She had gone, not wanting to leave that bedside and that voice, but once she stood on the stage in front of the hushed crowd, she thought of her mother's confidence and the tiny room where she had left her, and began to sing *A Mother's Love Is a Blessing*. It was an old familiar, perhaps too familiar, song, but in her absolute state of sincerity, the worn familiarity was turned into a solid rope of new gold. She carried the night, and her heart was fit to burst with possibility when she lifted the shield. Perhaps it would stop everything that seemed to be coming toward her; perhaps it might turn everything away from her mother. She was brimming with joy and bursting to go home and cheer up her sick mother and the house. She remembered the stunned silence in the hall as she finished. She sang it because her mother was sick, and because she had told her mother she would, and it had won the night by acclamation. She left to go as soon as she could, and she hurried home, but her mother had died while she was singing. She returned to a house of grieving, and she had her sister, three brothers, and a father to do it with, but no mother, and now, no voice. She had wanted to sing for a living, but now that was all gone, She would never sing like that again, for anyone.

She hadn't been by her mother when she died. She was away singing, *but she had,* but she had not—*but she had,* with her voice and her spirit—but mostly she was gone, and her breath and her tears and her panic at the loneliness of a world without a mother had almost overwhelmed her. Twelve years old, she wanted to run through the night, and still a part of her, over fifty years later, is running through that darkness still. I know that part of her well, because this young woman became my mother.

I know another part of her, too, that took the edge of that loss and sharpened it into an extraordinary compassion for others, an innate ability to sense loss and exile from the merest word or gesture. From a look or a silence. She never sang *A Mother's Love Is a Blessing* again in the whole of my growing, even though my sisters and I would ask her for it. "Go on, Mum, sing it now," we would say whenever we heard again the troubled story. But though she wouldn't sing, there was another sweet voice descanting behind her, an understanding of the way, no matter our successes, the world orphans each of us in turn. All through her life and the hard work of her life, she has shown a generous hospitality through the right word at the right time, for those without a sense of a home, a work, or a family in the world.

I vividly remember my sister's wedding. The meal being finished, my new brother-in-law rose to the occasion with glass in hand and, not known in his Yorkshire way for fine displays of sentiment or flights of praise, surprised us all by giving a moving and tender account of what he was gaining in this marriage. He took time to outline this woman's virtues; the difference she had made in his life, her tenderness, her care and compassion, and her willingness to invite him into her family. He started to tear up at the edges of sentences, his eyes moistening into a distant focus, barely held it together to the end of the speech, and sat down amidst thunderous applause with half the audience, including myself, in tears with him. The remarkable thing about this speech was that it was not spoken in celebration of my sister, his new wife, wonderful woman that she is. No, no, no. It was about Mary Theresa O'Sullivan, my mother, the young girl singing on the night of her mother's passing, looking out from the railing, sailing for England and now settled, after a lifetime of work, with three children in Yorkshire, and now, at last, becoming his new mother-in-law. My mother, through all her losses, has had that effect on people.

OUT OF IRELAND

I always feel the Yorkshire landscape of my childhood building before my eyes as I think about the inheritance of work, the mill chimneys standing against valley and moor, but there was another landscape and inheritance equally strong that breathed life into that vision of factory and field. The other half of my understanding of work and ambition was placed in a more imaginative realm by the influence of the young girl who had fled Ireland. She had left a motherless house and the gray and promiseless landscapes of post-war Ireland. Her inheritance was half of me, and it was the Irish in me that looked into my practical Yorkshire work world through a veil. On the other side of that veil was some kind of unarticulated and timeless friendship with loss and exile, with a shape-shifting world once a birthright of ancient but vague royalty from which we were all descended, now forgotten. All Irish, my mother would say with a laugh, were descended from kings—which, having looked into the matter since, is probably accurate, as it didn't take a great deal of land nor a great number of cows, to give their owners the grand title in ancient Ireland. But as children, this ever-present past gracing our humdrum working-class present seemed to create an invisible otherness in our growing.

This royal line felt like a thread of imaginative divinity run through our present accidental fetching up in a working-class York-shire household, as if in the details of everyday labor there was always some other world to remember. No matter how hard every-one had to work, there was an understanding that our place in the solid world is separated in only gossamer ways from greater and more eternal stories. In an Irish telling, like the telling of my mother's story, everything is ultimately experienced through terrible grief and loss. It is the one left singing, and the flight of song in the midst of that grief, that counts.

In my mother's youth, young Irish people, following an old migratory pattern familiar since the famine, left their families and emigrated all over the world. They were looking for work and I think also a freedom from the dead hand of postwar Ireland. Ironi-cally, the nearest place at hand was its old enemy, England, just a bus ride to Dublin and a boat ride across the Irish Sea. Prostrate as England was after the Second World War, it still had the ability to lure young women such as my mother to work in its grim factories and mills. "The bright lights," they would call it, and imagine it, before the disappointed shock of gray arrival. But any work was work, and any work that gave a modicum of independence to a constrained Catholic girl was a powerful magnet.

I shudder at the thought of that young woman in the gray, cold, bone-damp mornings of early-1950s Yorkshire. Few dances of a Saturday night, little music, food still rationed from the war, and her inherited lightness of tongue confronted by the stolid if friendly vowel sounds of Yorkshire dialect. *Young* was certainly the word to use—my mother was only fifteen, a scant three years from her mother's death, when she left to cross the water. After a long day's work in the woolen mills, she would still go and play in the local park like the young girl she was. I think of my own daughter's face with rising emotion when I remember my mother's story, how she had borrowed her sixteen-year-old sister's passport to leave her father's house.

My grandfather, in his grief at the prospect of her leaving him at such a young age, found and then hid the passport, fetching it out from behind a picture only after a night of weeping and pleading from his distraught daughter. Forty years later, the very day before that cottage was demolished, I leaned into the small room through the empty window frame and peered into the darkness. My mother pointed over my shoulder into the gloom to where the passport had stood on the mantle above the fire, and then to the chair in front of that fire where my grandfather had plunged a knife into the seat in grief and helplessness. I felt as if the knife were still upright in the

room, quivering with all the displaced power of the dispossessed.
The story is so Irish I want to weep myself at the thought of it—the
effervescent, temporary power of leave-taking and the powerlessness of those left behind.

FIGHTING FOR A LIVING

For all the powerlessness of my grandfather in that moment,
many of the O'Sullivan men on my mother's side were fighters and
boxers. If I ever think that a life of speaking and reading on the road
is a little tough, I have only to think of my great-grandfather who
went from village to village in his youth, fighting local challengers
for cash. The battering I take in the airport must count as nothing to
the grim determination he must have needed. He faced an inex-
haustible supply of young men appearing every day out of nowhere
and determined, literally, to make their mark in the world.

Two of my mother's other brothers were boxers and fought
regularly in the ring. My uncle John even appeared on television
when I was a child. I knew early on, and quite literally, that you
might have to fight for your living. I remember my uncle John on his
surprise visits to the house, bobbing and weaving above my young
head as he took the time to show me the boxer's crouch. My small
dukes circled forever in front of his huge, intent face, but I was too
mesmerized and worshipful ever to think of landing a blow. His
godlike presence was a great inspiration to a young would-be tough
guy. Part of me is still looking up, wondering whether I could ever
have the temerity to take my chance.

But sacrosanct as his own image is to me, he did teach me to love a good fight. The O'Sullivan in me may explain why I enjoy robust verbal encounters. The thrust and parry of argument, the stiletto jab of truth finally slipping beneath the unguarded verbal defense. It's not my normal mode of working, but there is a certain zest to that sudden threshold encounter. You suddenly know, in the midst of the verbal fight, that whatever is said in the heat of it can make or break everything, like a worthwhile marital argument, into something new and useful and revelatory. Many a time I have felt my uncle John very close to me over the years, looking over his gloves, urging me on in rough situations.

I do remember one work fight that began with an insult, a direct insult from a manager at a very large company. I was shocked at what he called me, and so was the rest of the room. It's a rare moment in any organization when someone picks a very public fight in a very public place and in such a vehement way. It *was* a moment of truth. The man was not only attacking me but the whole educational initiative within the company of which I was a part.

There was a lovely, important silence in the room when it happened. It was right at the end of the session, and many of the participants, though making a show of gathering their things to leave, were absolutely riveted as to the outcome and listening to find out just which way the current would go. You could also sense that a number were holding their breaths, wondering whether to follow him in turning against the course. It was perfect, really— one of the inherited difficulties in this organization was a lack of clear confrontation, a lack they said they were beginning to tackle. As a manager, you expected to be humiliated at one time or another by those who had seniority over you. The humiliation would then be "forgotten" and glossed over, so long as you remembered, of course, the underlying lesson.

I do believe in dignity and the preservation of personal honor. I believe in dignity; not in dignity's old shadow of puffery and self importance, but in its power to keep us true to our own spirit. With dignity comes honesty and an unwillingness to sell yourself short, to temporize or collude in cowardly ways that may preserve our jobs but not our honor. There are certain things we should not do, certain people we should not work for, lines we should not cross, conversations to which we should not descend, money we should not earn however easily it may come, things we should not allow ourselves to be called in public.

I didn't work for him and I wasn't beholden, and I felt my O'Sullivan dukes going up. I didn't insult him and I didn't belittle him, but in very short order he didn't care for my uncompromising reply, nor for a few sharp, stinging, and very satisfying knuckle-hard observations with my left while he was mesmerized with my more diplomatic right. I asked him why he wasn't prepared to ask some serious questions of my work in the session instead of ducking the issue and trying to humiliate me. He ignored me and turned to leave. I said he couldn't leave, he had called me a very bad name and now we had a relationship (definitely Irish humor). Also, what was he doing wasting his valuable time as a senior executive, only half participating in a program that was supposed to be voluntary? He stopped, and looked a little shocked. I wasn't playing the game of hierarchical acquiescence. In the background, I heard some interior voice humming the first line of an old Irish triad: *"Death to mock a poet . . ."*

Somewhere else in the background, my uncle John was circling, eyes bobbing behind the red gloves, jabbing and feinting. He was indicating the right glove, winking, and telling me to move in and give him a belting. After a while, under sustained hammering questions, he retreated down the corridor, but I followed him, inviting him to a real and respectable conversation on the matter. I wasn't sure who'd be out of the program, him or me, but an honest conversation seemed much more important than the outcome, and my blood was up. A whole crowd of managers followed us on their way to lunch. But our belligerent and bullying manager took flight, both in the encounter and, literally, next morning, from the building. He left the seminar; then, shortly after that, he left the company. I remember mostly regrets, wishing the confrontation had brought us to more of an understanding. But it was all for the best in the end for everyone else's participation. Certainly, from his point of view, he wasn't wasting his time any longer.

Afterward, a strange compliment came my way, which embarrassed me at first but which I later realized was a kind of Oscar nomination in corporate America. There were really two compliments. The first compliment was the refreshing enthusiasm for the course by those attending in succeeding months, who had heard of the encounter and who seemed to feel some old, tiresome, miasmic spell had been broken. It seemed to be a signal that there was something real about the seminar, something in earnest about the change effort. But a second compliment came more strangely to my ears, when I heard a warning circulating around the company, spoken earnestly to those about to join the course. The first time I heard the warning was in the following month. I said to a colleague after my seminar, "They seemed extraordinarily attentive this time."

"Whatever you do," he said, looking sideways at me, *"don't f—with the poet."* Then he put back his head and broke into laughter. "Don't *what?"* I said, and asked him for an explanation. This was the advice in the executive suites for those signing up for the next month's course. I was shocked, but then I had to laugh, too. Afterward, I felt a strange glow equal to that of seeing a book I'd written, long in the writing, out in the world for the first time. *Don't f— with the poet,* I said to myself repeatedly in some satisfaction as I drove away. I could almost see it in neon, emblazoned above the company production lines.

You could also say, *"Don't f— with the imagination,"* or with the one life we've been given, or with the gritty inheritance of our own ancestry, which we bring unknowingly to our work every day and whose ancient lineaments of belonging, poetry is constantly attempting to articulate. There is too much at stake, and we represent too long a lineage of lives lived and half lived who are cheering us on. Our work is a measure not only of our own lives but of all those who came before us and created the world we inherit. I hope they did not labor, starve, bear innumerable children, nor cross oceans to make a new life so we could give it all up in the promised land by some bland acquiescence to corporate career safety. I, for myself, remember the image of my uncle John, hovering over me, his dark O'Sullivan eyes emerging from above the gloves now and again, in effect, telling me not to be afraid of losing a fight. It is the dignity we keep, win or lose, which ennobles the confrontation. There he was, the latest of a long line of fighting Irish, transplanted invisibly into a corporate seminar room in North America to help me in an hour of peril. God love him. We need a few more of him.

THE HOPES OF OUR ANCESTORS

Each of us has some kind of tenacious family ancestry to call on in our work. No matter the glass and steel look of our office, somewhere in each of our backgrounds lies a layered, gritty complexity, an inheritance of people who came through. Life is too difficult to survive without tenacity and perseverance, and we all hold an unbroken thread of survivorship by the very fact that we are here, the latest in a very long line of survivors. Some of our ancestors were dogged, silent, and inarticulate in their holding on, some courageously outspoken, but imagine their disappointment in each of us, looking from the perspective of the particular heavens they inhabit, when we do not take another step for them. When we do not make a frontier of our own lives. If they were quiet in their own lives, they must want us to speak out; if they were loud and vociferous, they must want us to be more tempered and wiser with the fire, but none of them, surely, can stomach our willingness to hide ourselves in a bland compliance to powers or careers to which we have made ourselves slaves.

In my own ancestry, I descend, on both sides of my family, from a long line of the oppressed, dispossessed and marginalized, especially on the Irish, Scot, and Yorkshire side of my family, many of whom would be astounded to see the princely luxury and possibility of my contemporary life. I am but one generation away from this inheritance. Yet I do not see for their part, looking at their lives as prizefighters, fisherfolk and field laborers, any less of a sense of belonging to the world. They were simply joined to the conversation through the medium of want and difficulty. This want did not in any way reduce their rich inheritance of song, story, dialect and humor. I am, for my part, still trying to live up to a legacy they bestowed which is the fabric of my own life. My own struggle is to ensure that my present riches do not deracinate this gritty, ancestral and intuitive struggle.

THE BOUNDARIES OF PERSONAL POWER

When we are young, we imagine that we are doing everything ourselves. We have our work because we deserve it. We believe that we generate our own opportunities, our own luck, our own unstoppable bodies. There must be something to this, we intuit, that our fate varies according to those powers of attention which we bring to the frontiers of our young lives. But as we grow older, we grow wiser as to the extent of those powers; there is another, profounder way, in which we are dependent not only in invisible ways on the inheritance of others but literally and physically on what we have been given by those who have gone before us.

HELPING HANDS

We would stand barely a chance in the world if we did not rely from cradle to grave on what has been handed down from those who have lived and worked before us. From agriculture to health care, from education to sanitation, we are the recipients of generations of toil. I think of Richard Thorpe in 1667, founding Mirfield

Grammar School *"for fifteen poor children,"* a place whose doors I entered 300 years later at eleven years old, and where I was lucky enough to meet teachers both passionate and rigorous about what it meant to be a live, educated human being. I think of the library in Mirfield, a product of boring Victorian good works, but the scene of my first passionate encounter with real literature. Under a high shelf, I reached up tiptoe and pulled down my first book of adult poetry. Reading it, I felt as if I had been plucked from the ground by a passing hawk. A staid, century-old charitable contribution working its way like a wild animal into the intensity of my young life. Someone's fleeting image of a future world finding a nest in my growing imagination.

Sooner or later we admit that we cannot do it all, that whatever our contribution, the story is much larger and longer than our own, and we are all in the gift of older stories that we are only now joining. Whatever our success at work, in the financial markets, or in the virtual worlds now being born, we are all in the gift of much older work, we are all looked after by other eyes, and we are only preparing ourselves for an invitation to join something larger.

At my birth, unknown to me, I joined the story of the young woman leaning on the ship rail, leaving the shores of Ireland at a mere fifteen. But I spent a lot of my late teens and early twenties in a self-centered, invulnerable boy-god phase, sure I was master of the universe in which I lived. No one had come before me, no one would come after me, and I was certain that I was sole generator of my work, my gifts and my luck. My mother would be left far behind in my glorious wake and surely now could be no real contributor to a young warrior's prowess in the work and the world he had chosen for himself.

INVULNERABILITY AND INHERITANCE

This delusion of self-sufficiency came to an end in my mid-twenties. Firstly, with a humbling experience at a broken foot-bridge in the high Himalayas; secondly by a raging, hallucinatory bout of amebic dysentery a little farther along that mountain path; but thirdly, finally and thoroughly, sitting in an armchair back in Yorkshire, sipping a late-night whiskey with my mother. All the revelations of the Himalayas had only filled my cup to the very brim. It was my mother's words dropping from nowhere that filled it to overflowing.

Looking back, I remember it as a particularly haunting moment. I mean, mothers are not something to which a young man gives much thought in his work life, especially if his work takes him out in to the world in a venturesome way, and I had been venturing with a full, young, and masculine vengeance: rock climbing, ice climbing, sailing, traveling, and working on a shoestring budget through all the byways of the world. I had come through any number of near scrapes, had been attacked, shot at, or set on by dogs in all the best places and had always emerged breathless, a little battered, but triumphant. One near-fatal event would follow another, and I began to see myself like one of Napoleon's favored generals, except God was *my* supreme commander, someone who had bestowed upon me, rightfully, more than my share of luck.

In the midst of all this good luck, and seemingly far from my mother, a near drowning in the Galapagos Islands shook me to the core but in some ways also confirmed my idea of personal invulnerability. I had emerged like all the other times, rocked back on my heels but fully alive, and with another tale to mark my divinely ordained, youthful presence in the world.

The backdrop to the story was dramatic: an amphitheater of rock and sea on a wild, lonely, wave drenched hunk of rock on the southern edge of the Galapagos named Hood Island. Imagine an enormous lava cliff with the southern ocean rolling huge breakers against its base. Imagine small, black, dragonlike lizards known as marine iguanas, riding those waves, and when the waves recede, see them clinging in an impossible way to the rock face. Imagine the air filled with the cries of sea birds and sea lions, and imagine you hear, every so often, a huge roaring sound from a rock platform below the cliff, where the waves tear up through a deep crack in the living rock.

It was in this place, far from my mother in her armchair, that I came to lead Matt Downing, fellow naturalist guide, and former citizen of the safer regions of Upstate New York, from the paths of guiding righteousness and into the paths of a near death experience. Matt and I were on top of those cliffs, the southern edge of the most southerly island in the chain, staring at the vast sway of the sea that stretches southward for several thousand miles to the Antarctic ice shelf. Here, the northward fetch of the sea flowing up from those frozen latitudes at last greets something solid and dense in an angry series of waves exploding against the cliffs below. If you let your imagination run over the enormous lonely ocean stretching to the limitless south, this could be a very frightening place for lurid contemplation. Particularly if you thought of the New Zealand boat catastrophically lost just a few years previously. They hit these southern cliffs in the middle of the night and their boat had broken apart in moments. It would have taken just a few seconds, I imagine, their vessel shattered and lost in the maelstrom created by the sea meeting the cliffs beneath us.

You could imagine it all right, how it could have happened. They had rounded the Horn 5,000 miles to the south, left the coast of Chile, and sailed the long northward Humbolt current, day after day, night after night, until they believed somewhere inside them that the ocean was limitless and land a mere aberration. An island surely an unlikely event that they would approach only in full daylight as if in a dream. Their reckoning might be slightly out, their vigilance diminished. Perhaps in foul weather they could not see or feel the loom of the island, the sound of the waves on the cliff lost in the general tumult, until the great dark mass was all around them.

Whatever the story, I could never look from this cliff without thinking of their fateful last moments. Surprised by the violence of it all, the hard, lacerating rocks, the cold, rushing saltwater, they were soon in the calm oblivion that awaits us all, which, despite the attempts of the religious imagination, we still know nothing about. When I stood on that equatorial cliff, I felt as if I were on the frontier between north and south, life and death, substance and nothingness.

SETTING THE SCENE: THE ALBATROSS

North and south, life and death, substance and nothingness; there is one particularly magnificent creature who inhabits this exhilarating frontier between all those points. Hood Island is the chief nesting place of the waved albatross, a creature with an everlasting eight-foot wingspan which can stay aloft in the air for days or weeks at a time. If you want an image of tireless, effortless work, it would be this white creature, yellow-beaked, skimming the surfaces of the southern ocean, plucking fish from the crests of waves, alive to the enormous sway and swing of the fluid medium racing beneath it. One moment seen at the top of a cliff of waves, the next in the pit between them. When it does eventually come to land, it finds its way here, to Hood Island, to breed and to fish for the young that are hatched. Every March, the waved albatross congregate in their thousands on the cliff top, clashing their beaks together in a ritual of recognition and courtship, then they lay their eggs promiscuously in the open, rolling them around every now and again from place to place. There is a raffish edge to the albatross, a kind of devil-may-care involvement at the edge of things that is both amusing and breathtaking. It reaches a climax when the young come to fly. For weeks after hatching, the young albatross resemble great balls of fluff, their juvenile down permitting only their beaks and feet to jut out from the white mass that engulfs them. Then, as they molt, the shape of the bird emerges, ungainly but clearly an albatross.

What happens next is all of a piece with my story and my theme of work, and at the time seemed to give me a frightening glimpse into the subterranean life-and-death urgencies of Galapagos. The place continuously brought to the surface the merciless dynamics of life seemingly larger than any human morality. I might have been working in those islands but the islands themselves were working to some other, more frightening order. Every day in those islands, I glimpsed things I might have preferred to forget. In this case, the invulnerable flight of the albatross across the perilous waves emerged from an earlier and more frightening vulnerability.

Though the albatross is untouchable in its flight once launched into the wind, it has a very hard time actually getting off and away in the air due to its weight and size. It needs either a good breeze to lift it from the chop or a large cliff from which to propel itself. For the young albatross coming to maturity, the only way into the air was over the huge cliff that lay to one side of where they had hatched. Every one of the thousands of albatross chicks had but one chance in their short lives to learn to fly.

It was heart-stopping to watch the rotund birds stagger toward that abyss, slowly pick up speed, and then suddenly stop themselves at the edge, practicing for the fateful launch. I would see them, day after day, lumbering back away from the cliff, their heads swaying purposefully and distinctively from side to side. Some inner evolutionary conviction pushing them into this all-or-nothing leap.

I remember looking down from that cliff one still day without a breath of wind in the air, a day, unfortunately, the growing birds had responded to some inner urgency to try at last. All along the bottom of the cliff lay the bodies of young albatross I had seen come to maturity in the previous months. All that growing come to nothing. The nesting areas now silent and empty of familiar birds I had come to recognize despite their fluffy anonymity. Without the help of a breeze, they had not cleared the rocks below and their white bodies had smashed into the jutting lava, littering the whole length of the shoreline. White ragged piles on the black lava. A few, a very few, had made it; they were floating with their elders out on the waves, survivors who would carry their skills into the limitless ocean. In their bodies were hidden the wellsprings of talent that would flood into the next generation. It was a fierce but exhilarating sight, one that would make me, nevertheless, question God's way of going about things. You had to ask yourself what equivalent, seemingly merciless urgencies, informed our own human world.

THE BLOWHOLE

At one point beneath that cliff lay the large platform of lava rock. A ramp in the cliff led down onto the platform, and if you followed it you could get a close look at the frightening undercut cliff below. It also led you to the source of the regular roaring sound, a roaring you could hear the whole length of the shoreline. A huge, curving crack snaked in from the edge of the cliff for twenty feet; beneath this, the full fury of the ocean would concentrate before spraying up through the opening to a height of about thirty or forty feet above the platform. The whole effect was like witnessing Yellowstone's famous geyser, Old Faithful. There was even a similar shape to the plume and a similar comforting regularity. As a guide, I would take people to see this blowhole, and more often than not I would stand near the edge of the crack and take a saltwater shower under the falling plume, while the group I was leading clicked merrily away, capturing the moment for their slide shows. I had done this for months, and I was sure it had helped increase the generosity of the group when, at journey's end, they held a collection for the guide's deserving tip.

In this spirit I persuaded my fellow guide, Matt, to join me at the edge of the blowhole. He was a little hesitant, but soon joined in the exhilaration of being showered by the scattered tons of water falling on us from a great height. I remember seeing the photographs many weeks later, taken by the watching group one moment before disaster struck. There we are, framed forever, having all the fun in the world. But beneath us, off camera, in the midst of the fun, the water suddenly disappeared. There was an eerie moment as we watched the water gurgle away down the crack and then waited for it to surge back again. It did not. The water went away and stayed away. Something was wrong. I looked out to the sea below. There the ocean was curling itself up into the most frightful, pent-up tsunami of water. I grabbed Matt's arm and shouted, "God Almighty!" We barely had time to turn away when the mighty surge barreling back up the crack was overtaken by the huge wave itself rolling over the top of the cliff. Caught in the maelstrom, I remember trying to keep my feet up in front of me, because there was a twelve-foot rock step in the platform against which we were being flung. I didn't want to hit it head-first. My arm had been loosed from Matt's, and he was off, disappearing into the surging nothingness. I hit the lava wall feet-first, thank God, and then we were dragged back by the force of the ebbing water over the platform to the very edge of the cliff. The next image offered to the eyes of our watching group was myself, gripping the edge of the blowhole, my feet hanging down into its mouth as if into some engulfing creature, scrambling to stay out of its throat. Beyond me, Matt hung off the edge of the cliff itself, his feet swinging wildly for purchase. The next wave hit us like a hammer blow. This time there was no keeping my feet in any direction. In the savage onslaught I was somersaulted toward the step, over and over. I could almost feel the coming concussion. It never came; the second wave was so huge that it took me right over the top of the lava step. I surged forward, banging against the rocks, until I reached the awestruck group, where I was left at their feet by the retreating water, lacerated and shocked.

I remember looking up into the horrified faces and thinking in an abstract way that this performance should merit a very large tip. The thought crumpled immediately in the shock and realization of my banged-up state. I was also desperate for a sight of Matt. I looked along the platform. There he was. Thankfully, he had cleared the step and lay about thirty feet away, blood running down his back and arms. We were taken hurriedly back to the landing place, Matt evacuated to his mother ship, deliriously asking if anyone got the number of the truck that hit him, while I recovered myself lying flat out on the beach, amazed that I wasn't as bad, or worse, or dead.

STRUCK DOWN

What is left in my memory is the sheer quivering power of the ocean that day. Its power was even more unsettling because as soon as the second wave had gone, the sea returned to its regular rhythm and the blowhole to its original contained fury. A freak wave, two freak waves, near destruction, and then a return to shocked normality. I had heard about them, waves out of nowhere, even in the midst of the ocean, turning boats over, but I had never witnessed them firsthand. It was as if the hand of the sea had reached out, sensing some arrogance on its borders, and given me the merest touch of its pure potentiality. I lay on the landing beach with a deep pain running through my stomach. I had been struck to the core, as if my insides had been rearranged, as if touched by a god in a Greek drama. In the old Greek stories depicting fleeting encounters with divinity, the touch of a god was always experienced as both violation and blessing. The violation was in my stomach—someone had reached inside me and in no uncertain terms informed me that I was like everything else in the world, I had no immunity. The blessing came in an unconscious physical respect for the sea that began to inform everything I did around the boats, from the merest tying of a knot to the safety of every individual and group in my care.

The blessing was also in sheer survival. A few feet here, a few feet there, and I would have been over that cliff, from whence there was no return. A boat could not have even approached the place to pick up my body. I felt I had been given the sight of my own end and had returned to carry the revelation into the rest of my existence. This notion of my own vulnerability had something to do with belonging to the world like everything and everybody else. I was not a discrete sports star in the firmament of my own adulation. I belonged to everything, and everything had its own life equal to my own, and its own ending. Still, in an ironic way, I felt sure that I had come to all this myself, under my own luck and power.

PLUCKED FROM THE WAVES

As the waves recede, I come, three years later, to the armchair in Yorkshire and my mother sipping whiskey. The Jamieson's was a sweet accompaniment to a late-night, bittersweet talk. I was home for only a short stay, and we were talking about my travels and the amount of time I spent away from her. In inimitable Irish fashion, my mother was telling me how much she missed me, how she thought about me every day and said a prayer to herself for my safety every night. The old *beannacht,* the Irish power of blessing, welling under her late-night words. I nodded in good son-like fashion but was ready to move on to other more adult things, appropriate to a grown man talking with his mother. But before I could encourage the conversation onto other ground, she began to tell me about a vivid dream she had woken from during my time in the Galapagos, three years before.

Apparently, in the dream I had been standing on a black cliff with one other person, next to a fountain of water. A huge, frightening wave bore down on us in the dream. *The blowhole on Hood Island.* The hair stood up on the back of my neck as she spoke, describing in clear detail from her dream the exact circumstance of my near drowning. I had never so much as breathed a word of the incident, knowing how much she worried about me at the best of times, nor had I told my father or either of my sisters. "You were standing on the cliff edge next to the strange fountain when a big wave came over the top and swept you away. You came floating back in all the turmoil but then another bigger wave came and you were being taken out to sea. I felt the blackness of the water waiting for you. In the dream I leaned down from above and took hold of you by the back of the neck. I lifted you out and put you safely back on the cliff. When I woke I felt so happy that I had been able to save you."

I looked at my mother with total amazement. The hair rising on my neck and the shiver in my spine had little to do with the Jamieson's which I had to put down. I was shocked into silence to hear such a precise description of something so private to me, a clear description of the frightening trauma I had been trying, I realized, to forget, faraway on that lonely shore. The sound of the waves seemed to surround me as she spoke, the smoke of the sea spray thundering amidst the bird cries. I looked at her as if I had seen a ghost, which I had. It was my self-image disappearing into a wraith-like form and leaving me forever. I told my mother the other side of the story. We stared into our glasses; we looked at each other.

From somewhere inside the fearful memory, I felt a level of absurdity about the whole thing, about my pretensions and the sense I had of my own powers. I found myself amidst other waves, waves of laughter, laughter at the folly of it all. They began to ripple to the surface, and my mother began to laugh, too.

"Bloody marvelous, isn't it?" I said. "Here I am adventuring around the world like some invulnerable version of Indiana Jones, lord of all I survey, and all the time it is my bloody mother coming in like the cavalry at the end and saving me from the jaws of the destruction." We raised the glasses together, hooting at the image. But as the laughter subsided, I found myself telling myself in no uncertain terms, *David, whatever it is you think you are, give it up. There are powers at play in the world about which you know very little. Like, for instance, this little woman sitting in front of you, who sponsored your exclusive membership in this hard-to-obtain world and for all you know still pays a hefty part of your annual dues.*

There was a definite feeling in the room of time stopping dead still, of the veil being torn from our ordinary perceptions of time and space, here and there, then or now. I'm not interested in the psychic glamour of it all, or the intuitive reach of my mother, which I had experienced many times before. Yes, I was perfectly prepared to believe that the intercession was real, that without her watchful, loving presence I would have been swept away, never to be seen again. But irrespective of the far-fetched reality of it all, something else had happened inside me while the conversation proceeded that night. I stopped trying to do it all myself. I was like everything else in this life. I didn't need to have absolute total control over my destiny. I couldn't have it anyway. It was ridiculous to try. It was all right if I lived in a world in which my mother had saved me in the end.

In the shock of hearing my mother tell me my closely held and secret trauma, I was given a sense of the intimate way everything is a brother and sister to everything else. Everything we see as private is somehow already out in the world. The singularity of existence is only half the story; all of our singularities are in conscious and unconscious conversation with everything else. The fierce ecologies of belonging I had witnessed in Galapagos extended in and through my own body, like a long wave-form passing right through my life. My uncle John was passing through my life, my mother was passing through my life, all my ancestors were still passing through my life. Sitting there in front of the fire of a damp Yorkshire evening, I felt as if these waves of revelation and belonging had at last come to claim me like the Pacific breakers had once tried. As physical and real an experience as it had seemed living in Galapagos, I had only slowly been soaking in the truth of the place. It took going home again, and meeting the intensely personal and physical creature reality of my mother.

Mother is probably one of the more incontrovertible truths of life, not amenable to masculine theory. As men, we have no immediate notion of creating another being from our own bodies, of having that part of you grow and go out in the world while still remaining forever you, or that you could trace that reality even in absence like a lost limb while the body still feels it is present. There I sat, poleaxed in front of my own mother, birthed again into a larger world, looking out from my dad's armchair in the house in which I grew to maturity. The true *armchair* adventurer.

AMBITION AND ANCESTRAL IMAGINING

Whatever powers we have in the world, in our work, in our powers of leadership, in our imaginations, they are in the gift of a much larger world than one we have made for ourselves. They are only a part of deeper, inescapable, ancestral imaginings which we join and which inform our every day and to which, every next day, we introduce our own children. More truthfully, perhaps, we let our children go out in the world and find it all for themselves, and report it back to us as if new—late one night, perhaps, with an inspirational bottle of something or other next to the fire. But the act of *knowing* and remembering this larger story, as we watch them grow, changes everything. Our presence in their lives changes everything when our actions are part of a larger story. We stop informing our children, consciously or unconsciously, that in the world of work, their own powers or their own career goals alone will bring them happiness.

As I think about it, my mother's absolute confidence in me as a child, whatever I chose to do in the world, was probably the basis upon which I could venture so confidently into the world. It must have come from her own knowledge of the precarious nature of life, the loss of her mother, and her fleeing from the blustering, shad-owed authority of 1940s Catholic Ireland. The leave-taking, the crossing of the short but still unknown Irish Sea to make a home in a foreign land, sharpened her perceptions of the individual nature of every given life. She has never said it out loud; she has always lived it out loud.

There is another coda to my mother's childhood and to the strange ways our particular childhoods are handed down generation to generation. Whatever sense I have of my own identity as a man, there is a part of me forever singing my heart out like a young girl while my mother lies dying in bed. A part of me shyly stepping onto a stage in Ireland in the late 1940s. There is also a part of me, for all my singing of poetry and prose, that will not sing that one song again. In a parallel world there is a part of me, hands half frozen, fishing for silver clouds of herring in the North Sea, as my father's family did at the end of the nineteenth century. What other unspoken stories and lives live on in each one of us, in our work, in our imaginings? We are the ending of some stories, the carrying on of others, and often just the beginning of many it is not our place to finish.

Here at least, is the end of one particular story, told in this chapter, and the beginning, perhaps, of other stories yet to be spoken. A few years ago, my mother traveled to the United States to see me and to warm the old house I had just bought and renovated to share with my son. We sat on a couch on the bare but beautifully polished planked floor, with my neighbor and friend, Peggy. I played a few Irish tunes on the violin for my mother, and then we talked about the new home and drank a glass or so to its future. We talked homes, all the houses and homes we had known. We talked of settling into homes, making homes, leaving homes. But Peggy's attention was caught and riveted when she found that my mother had lost her mother at exactly the same age she had lost her own. You could sense the electricity in the air between them. Quiet but crackling. Old longings and embers of loss, stirred, spoken, and above all understood. Peggy quietly asked my mother how she had taken her mother's death. My mother told her about the night of the singing competition, how she had sung that song, won, and never sung it again. There was another, longer silence. Peggy asked even more quietly, "Would you sing it for me?" I said nothing, I waited, I watched without breathing. My mother looked at Peggy. I could see her seeing Peggy, seeing herself at the same age, motherless in the world. She looked down for a second, she cleared her throat, and out of nowhere, damn it, she began to sing.

A Mother's Love Is a Blessing filled our new house, the notes clear and bright in the uncluttered room. I looked at that lined but beautiful face lifted like a bird, and listened to the song unsung for forty-six years, wishing my sisters could be brought invisible, to witness it. The song ended. I walked over to my violin laid on the table. I put it under my chin and started up a reel. My mother stood up, put her arms down by her sides, kicked off her shoes, and in small light, unbroken steps danced sprightfully across the room to the tumbling notes, while Peggy clapped, as light and graceful and innocent as the girl she had been.

Arrivals

VI

The Awkward Way the Swan Walks:

FROM EXHAUSTION TO WHOLEHEARTEDNESS

We are are forever in the midst of beginnings and arrivals: the child's tiny crumpled face, looking out from its white, linened nest; the bowed heads of green buds beneath the Hawthorn, just about to open into color. We are just as compelled and caught by endings and departures: the deathbed hand held in ours, its parchment transience grazing ours, just as it seems to be closing into something definite and sure. Out of birth comes anticipation and imagination; out of death and leaving we are given lit memories and stark sorrow, haloed by significance. The three year old becomes the thirty-year-old becomes the three-times-thirty-year-old becomes an ancestor to our own years, their work strangely forgotten while their face is clear in our memory. We work in the midst of all these beginnings and endings. We coast past the silent blue ambulance lights on the freeway and complete our commute in the midst of dying and loss. Through the seasons we cut sandwiches, chop celery, wipe two-year-old noses, put together formidable business plans, and hold important meetings. All the while, life arrives and departs as we labor.

Most of our days we do not perceive beginnings and endings; births and deaths feel blessedly far away, we find ourselves almost always in the middle of things. Sometimes for years we seem to be nothing but middle. Middle and muddle. Real beginnings and real departures seem a distant memory, and after a long time without the rawness of those firsthand experiences, they become something we are not sure we want anymore, something we want to hold at bay.

> *What fortitude the Soul contains,*
> *That it can so endure*
> *The accent of a coming Foot,*
> *The opening of a Door!*
> —EMILY DICKINSON

The door does open, the footfall turns into a person, the person enters our fragile aloneness. It is a neighbor, a colleague, or a death, come to us at last, no middle lasts. More to the point for the raw, poetic imagination of someone like Emily Dickinson, no middle is really any middle at all. For someone who lived her life mostly behind closed doors, Emily Dickinson understood the nature of constant visitation.

> *I dwell in Possibility—*
> *A fairer House than Prose—*
> *More numerous of Windows—*
> *Superior—for Doors—*
> *Of Chambers as the Cedars—*
> *Impregnable of Eye—*
> *And for an Everlasting Roof—*

The Gambrels of the Sky—
Of Visitors—the fairest—
For Occupation—This—
The spreading wide of narrow Hands
To gather Paradise—

Paradise, to Emily, is sheer presence, something she can harvest with her own hands; presence is faith, and faith is the ability to
pay attention to the world according to *how* we are made. The depth
of our identity is dependent upon the depth of our attention. Real
attention to our work opens up all the births and deaths constantly
attendant on its doing and undoing. Middle may seem real, but
middles are fleeting, mostly illusory, a form of defense. Life arrives
and departs in the middle. All our great artistic and religious traditions take great pains to tell us so. Middle barely exists. Everything
is being born and is being borne up even as it is simultaneously
dying and falling. Nothing is at rest, only in fleeting restful harmony
like a single snowflake seen through a window, descending with all
the others until it is reimagined again and again by time, temperature, and wind. But the illusion of middle is comfort; middle can be
wonderful insulation; middle is good—until it comes to an end,
which is always sooner than we had hoped.

IN THE MIDDLE OF MAGNIFICENCE

When you look in the world atlas for the city of Seattle, you
find it nestled in the very top left-hand corner of the United States,
right up against the Canadian border, sitting at the edge of an inland

sea. The map indicates the name of the sea, *The Puget Sound*. Look more closely and you see the sound is specked with islands and that the city, the sound, and the islands are surrounded by mountains. To the right, you can trace one of those mountain ranges, the Cascades, sweeping up the spine of the American West Coast, just brushing the city's eastern boundary on its way up into Canada. On the left side of the map, west of the city and the islands in the sound, lies the other bounding range, the white, roadless wilderness of the Olympic Mountains.

Three mountains stand out higher on the map than any others. Mount Rainier in the south, Mount Baker in the north, and Mount Olympus in the center of the Olympics to the west. If you formed a triangle from these mountains and gazed into the center of that triangle, you would find yourself looking at one island in particular—a long, wandering island snaking north and south that opens into a teardrop at its southern end. At the eastern edge of this teardrop, there is a small town close to the shore. If you could, in your mind's eye, look even closer beyond the details of the map, you would find in that seaside town an old wooden building full of many offices, and in one of these offices, in the mid-eighties, you would have found a very busy man oblivious to every bit of magnificence you had seen surrounding him on the map.

Ten years after my time in the Galapagos, this wooded island in the Pacific Northwest had become my home. Ten years after Galapagos, I found myself still attempting to turn my love affair with the natural world into a work, a life, and a job. The nonprofit institute I had found on the island seemed a perfect vehicle. The organization was fine. *I* was in big trouble, trouble of my own making, busy all right, busy educating myself right out of any relationship with nature by the very way I was trying to bring it to others. There was an immense world outside my window that I was attempting to represent, but it was a world that was slowly receding from my physical experience exactly because of the way I tried to represent it. I looked, but I couldn't see anymore. I was suffering a form of self-inflicted amnesia.

BUSINESS, BUSYNESS, AND SPEED

Amnesia of the imaginative kind always seems to stem from a form of arrogance. My arrogance took the form of busyness. I was incredibly busy. I had lots of responsibility, lots of meetings, courses to run, people to accommodate, budgets to meet. My blue-water, carefree life in the Galapagos islands was but a distant memory. I had learned to work very fast, barely stopping for anything that did not seem productive or an aid to production. I moved from photocopier, to receptionist, to filing cabinet in a tight, self-enclosed orbit. Speed was my essence and, I thought, my true savior in solving the difficulties of commitment and the increasing burden of detail.

Speed in work has compensations. Speed gets noticed. Speed is praised by others. Speed is self-important. Speed absolves us. Speed means we don't really belong to any particular thing or person we are visiting and thus appears to elevate us above the ground of our labors. When it becomes all-consuming, speed is the ultimate defense, the antidote to stopping and really looking. If we really saw what we were doing and who we had become, we feel we might not survive the stopping and the accompanying self-appraisal. So we don't stop, and the faster we go, the harder it becomes to stop. We keep moving on whenever any form of true commitment seems to surface. Speed is also warning, a throbbing, insistent indicator that some cliff edge or other is very near, a sure diagnostic sign that we are living someone else's life and doing someone else's work. But speed saves us the pain of all that stopping; speed can be such a balm, a saving grace, a way we tell ourselves, in unconscious ways, that we are really not participating.

The great tragedy of speed as an answer to the complexities and responsibilities of existence is that very soon we cannot recognize anything or anyone who is not traveling at the same velocity as we are. We see only those moving in the same whirling orbit and only those moving with the same urgency. Soon we begin to suffer a form of amnesia, caused by the blurred vision of velocity itself, where those things germane to our humanity are dropped from our minds one by one. We start to lose sight of any colleagues who are moving at a slower pace, and we start to lose sight of the bigger, slower cycles that underlie our work. We especially lose sight of the big, unfolding wave form passing through our lives that is indicative of our central character. On the personal side, as slaves to speed, we start to lose sight of family members, especially children, or those who are ill or infirm, who are not flying through the world as quickly and determinedly as we are. Just as seriously, we begin to leave behind the parts of our own selves that limp a little, the vulnerabilities that actually give us color and character. We forget that our sanity is dependent on a relationship with longer, more patient cycles extending beyond the urgencies and madness of the office.

A friend falls sick, and in that busyness we find their interruption of our frantic lives frustrating and distracting. On the surface we extend our sympathies, but underneath we are already moving in a direction that takes us far away. We flee the situation even if we are sending flowers every day; we rejoin, thankfully, the world that is on the go, on the move, untouched by mortality. Once we ourselves are touched by that mortality, however, through whatever agency it arrives in our lives—a broken limb, the loss of a loved one, the collapse of our business, a moment of humiliation in the doorway of a meeting room—our identities built on speed almost immediately fall apart and disintegrate. We find ourselves suddenly alone and friendless, strangers even to ourselves.

How Good Work Gets Done

We seem to have to learn about the illusions of speed individual by individual, generation after generation. Yet speed by itself has never been associated with good work by those who have achieved mastery in any given field. Speed does not come from speed. Speed is a result, an outcome, an ecology of combining factors in a person's approach to work; deep attention, well-laid and well-sharpened tools, care, patience, the imagination engaged to bring disparate parts together in one whole.

Here is Michael Finkel of *The Atlantic Monthly*, describing Steven Allen, Britain's champion dry stone waller, in the midst of a wall-building competition on the Yorkshire moors, looking at the elements which combine to produce speed as a marvellous by-product:

I watched Allen work. He'd stand stock-still for a moment and stare at his wall with a calculating look on his face. Then he would swiftly turn around and bend down and select a stone. He'd twist it and jiggle it and flip it over and back, as if fiddling with prayer beads. Then he'd pick up his hammer, hold the stone to his thigh, and chip off pieces with a few sharp taps. One of the qualities that sets Allen apart from other wallers is his feel for the hidden seams snaking through a rock. . . . When Allen hit a rock, it invariably fractured along a plane as smooth as a sail.

The right touch at the right time in the right place. The right word at the right time in the right place. Effort and will used only at pivotal moments. How we long for that deftness and that mastery, the ability to tap and cleave the fault lines of our own stubborn, stonelike working difficulties. To crack the stone like essence of our everyday work. But Allen's speed seems to arise from his ability to discern emerging patterns, even when most of the other competitors are making the mistake of putting speed first, sweating, and heaving their stones into place.

If he was setting [the stone] into a space between two others, the rock would literally click into place, wedged between its neighbors as tightly and neatly as if Allen were building with Lego bricks. He'd nod, reach down and sweep up the chips he'd broken off, and pack them into the center of the wall. Then he'd study the next gap for a second or two, spin around, and pick up another stone.

Moments of speed and urgency but dependent on a felt perception of the larger pattern. The ability to close on something and then let it go. The key seems to be to find a restful yet attentive presence in the midst of our work, to open up a spaciousness even in the center of our responsibility. To find some source of energy other than our constant applications of effort and will. If we attempt to engage the will continually, it exhausts us and prevents us from creating something with a pattern that endures. A well-built, dry stone wall such as Allen constructs, free of cement, can settle, move, adapt to temperature, and function as a good wall for hundreds of years. In the limestone areas of Yorkshire, there are walls dating to the twelfth century; in Ireland, the remains of some dry stone field walls are 4,000 years old.

As Finkel remarks, "Cement walls do not reach old age. Cement walls do not move. They crack, and then they fall. 'Cement,' Allen says, 'is a sin.'"

We might say, as we attempt to construct something enduring in our own lives, that speed is a sin as constraining as cement. Speed seems to speak of movement but it actually glues us into whatever immobile, unattending identity we have constructed. The moment we stop the constant willful building, the edifice of our work falls down.

Thinking on stone walls, I remember the long stone walls of a particular Welsh farm where I used to live and a particular old sheepdog that lived amongst those walls. The farm's name was Tan-y-Garth, and the dog's name was Cymro, which means Welshman. Cymro was Welsh through and through, from the tip of his black ear to the end of his tail, and looked on with deep respect as the best dog in the valley, which was saying something in that endless patchwork of sheep farms, particularly as John, Tan-y-Garth's owner, was known as a trainer of the very best caliber and someone who had brought along many a dog to give Cymro a run for his money. But Cymro never ran, he never needed to, and besides, he was far too old to do it. When I first came to know this grizzled, one ear up, one ear down, black-and-white genius, he was about thirteen years old, virtually blind in one eye, with a distinct limp in his right hind leg. While other, younger dogs took off in great curving runs up the sides of the mountain to move the sheep along, Cymro would simply limp behind the multitude of ragged backs and lean slightly toward them, showing the flock his good eye. With pinpoint accuracy, the sheep would pass straight through the gap in the wall where John wanted them to go. Cymro was a virtuoso, a Joe Montana of the dog world. He knew the pivotal places to stand, the pivotal ways to move; he occupied the center of the sheep universe and knew their collective minds even before they did; he barely ever broke into a lope. If I ever want to slow myself, I think of old Cymro's economy of presence. We might envy the energy of the young, but there is as much to envy in the learned simplicity of those who know the essential relationships well enough to do the job and to do it with the lightest touch.

SPEEDING TO A STOP

I was far from Cymro's effortlessness in the busy office building I had since made my home. Far from Wales, far from Galapagos. But all this increasing busyness was my unknowing way of covering up for the fact that I was not standing in the right pivotal place, not leaning in the right direction, not showing my good eye. Poetry tugged and beckoned to me to move in its direction, but I hadn't the faith for the final step of making myself visible. How was I to make a living from it, for God's sake? The question seemed to stop everything in its tracks. I kept moving, ignoring the whispered invitation. Speed, ironically, is so often a symptom of total immobility.

Besides, the reasons *not* to follow that particular pilgrim path were there in magnificent quantities. If you ever want ammunition to shoot down any secret ambition, ask others in an abstract kind of way what they think of your plans. We keep the most precious things secret exactly because we are not sure they would stand up to scrutiny in the light. A heartfelt desire is like a seed that needs the dark and the cold before it will germinate. The difficulty is that when spring eventually arrives, we can be so used to our desire being shelved in the dark that we keep it there and cover up the shoots even when the outer conditions for its growth may be right.

If you want to meet terrifying silence, tell the world you are going full-time as a poet. Who would give me a word of encouragement if I did? It has never been easy to go full-time as a poet in any recorded portion of human history. When we announce to the world that we are about to go full-time as a poet, people do not come up to us, slapping us on the back, saying, "Great career move, David," or "I hear they are taking them on at Lockheed right now," or "Marvelous. I hear there is a decent dental plan comes with the verse." Silence is the common response. Quite often they won't even give us the good grace of arguing. They think better of encouraging us by any sign, good or bad.

And there is, for those married or otherwise committed, another silence to be encountered, a silence far more spine-chilling than anything we may have encountered before: the uncomprehending, far-reaching silence of the father-in-law. The silence of the father-in-law goes beyond anything we have known. It is the part of you, now concentrated in this frowning, wordless face, that wants to know how spouse and child are to be fed, housed, educated, and given their next pair of inline skates. Father-in-law is difficult, difficult but good; he makes us real and accountable. He tells us the decision has to be made out of the fabric of our lives, and in relationship with others in that fabric, it will not be achieved by tearing everything apart.

But I didn't need father-in-law to stop me at this point. I was doing a fine job by myself. *If only I could go faster* was my main preoccupation. But leave anything badly built to itself, stop running around holding it up here and then there, and like a badly built dry stone wall, it falls down, which is what quickly happened. One morning, hurtling from my desk toward the photocopier, I passed a roomful of my colleagues just about to start a meeting. There was someone I needed to talk to. I saw immediately that he wasn't among them, but I put my head in the door before they could begin, and in a very loud, urgent voice, I said, "Has anyone seen David?"

There was a moment of stunned incomprehension, which to my amazement, quickly dissolved into table-thumping laughter. My comic timing must have been impeccable, because the whole room was soon helpless, repeating what I had said and generally behaving like the pig-ignorant fools other people seem to be when the joke is at our expense. I looked back at them blankly, the truth dawning as I looked. "Has anyone seen David" might seem an innocuous question in most organizations, but I happened to be the only David who worked under that particular roof. I realized the forlorn and public stupidity of my request and forced myself, after a wide-eyed moment, to laugh with them. Inside, I was dying.

LOOKING FOR DAVID

I was looking for David, all right, and I couldn't find him. In fact, I hadn't seen him for a very long time. I was looking for a David who had disappeared under a swampy morass of stress and speed.

In the humiliation of that moment, caught forever in a doorway, calling my own name, I saw I had become a stranger to myself. Not only that, but my self-exile had been revealed in a very public way. The workplace carries so much of our desperate need for acknowledgment, for hierarchy, for reward, to be seen, and to be seen as we want to be seen, that we often overreach ourselves, and our passionate and often violent inner needs suddenly break through the placid professional exterior. I obviously had a violent need to find myself and give myself a good talking-to. Everyone else in the office had discovered that at exactly the same moment as I had.

I stood in that doorway, before that small audience, in absolute humiliation, which as it turns out, was a very good thing. Humiliation is mostly something we try to avoid, but it is something more often, all for the best, in retrospect. There is a lovely root to the word, the Latin word *humus* meaning *soil* or ground. When we are humiliated, we are in effect returned to the ground of our being. Any fancy ideas we have about ourselves are shriven away by the reality of the moment. We come to earth with a thump. It may be a narrow dark piece of ground, but at least it is real and at least it is our own. I had suddenly got off the upward and onward, abstract ladder of work and come back to ground; David, the efficient Wizard of Oz work machine, had suddenly had the curtain whisked aside. I was astonished and agonized to see who was standing behind the veil.

Yeats says,

I must lie down where all the ladders start,
In the foul rag-and-bone shop of the heart.

When you get to the bottom, you'll find everything you've disowned and thrown away from yourself lying around on the ground. There was a lot of old familiar material to be seen. I was *looking for David* because I hadn't seen him for the longest time and I sincerely wondered where he was. I was *looking for David* because I had become a stranger to myself and didn't even have time for a snatched conversation about things that really mattered to me. I was *looking for David* because some inner relationship had been neglected and taken for granted; I had become like an old married couple who had stopped talking years before, the inner friendship with my old self slowly tearing apart under the strain. Behind the curtain was a man who was afraid to cross a threshold of visibility needed to make his place in the world.

THE HAUNTED HOUSE
OF INSIGNIFICANT SUCCESSES

The house I had built from my work was busy, but in the way a haunted mansion is busy, full of wails and rattling chains. All the time I refused to acknowledge my core work, I was turning myself into a ghost on the surface. Sooner or later the real living person has to flee the haunted house. The threshold of that meeting room was a difficult, visible place to come awake, but at least I had come round from the fevered night. I had woken from the night terror of busyness, calling my own name, a name that had sprung unconsciously to my lips. We always reveal ourselves in the end, especially under the pressures of work. Sometimes we reveal ourselves subtly, so subtly that we do not even know we have done it. But I had chosen to do it in public: I must have wanted to shout it from the rooftops.

"Has anyone seen David?"

He was here, and he was very, very tired. As I stood in the doorway of the meeting room, I felt the energy flow out of me for this work, like an aspiring actor who had been continually painting, not a character, but a portion of the background scenery. I knew all at once, I couldn't stay backstage anymore.

I wanted to step out from the scenery and bring myself into some sharp outline in the light, to become foreground instead of background. I wanted to step out into the footlights and cast my shadow on something grand. I was tired of background because I had become background. If I was an actor, I had at least made my debut in that doorway, even if I was playing the skull in the graveyard scene from *Hamlet*. Poor old Hamlet took one look at me and said, "Alas, poor Yorick! I knew him, Horatio: a fellow of infinite jest, of most excellent fancy . . ." My fancies had been excellent, all right, and my constant busyness the infinite jest. A killing tragicomedy of errors. I contemplated my faded vitality in that doorway as Hamlet contemplated Yorick's bony head, something that once had been alive and familiar years before, but now moldered and strangely come to light, seeming to belong mostly to the dead.

Part of the reason stopping seems like a death is that speed has become our core competency, our core identity. We do not know what powers we would be left with if we stopped doing what we were doing in the busy way we were doing it. Besides, there is a deeper, older human intuition at play that knows any real step forward comes through our pains and vulnerabilities, which is the reason we began to busy ourselves in the first place, so that we could stay well away from them. If we stopped, we would have to sojourn in areas that have nothing to do with getting things done but everything to do with being done to ourselves.

AWKWARDNESS AND VULNERABILITY

We have the strange idea, unsupported by any evidence, that we are loved and admired only for our superb strength, our far-reaching powers, and our all-knowing competency. Yet in the real world, no matter how many relationships may have been initiated by strength and power, no marriage or friendship has ever been deepened by these qualities. After a short, erotic honeymoon, power and omnipotence expose their shadow underbellies and threaten real intimacy, which is based on mutual vulnerability. After the bows have been made to the brass god of power, we find in the privacy of relationship that same god suddenly immobile and inimicable to conversation. As brass gods ourselves, we wonder why we are no longer loved in the same way we were at our first appearance. Our partners have begun to find our infallibility boring and, after long months or years, to find us false, frightening, and imprisoning.

We have the same strange idea in work as we do in love: that we will engender love, loyalty, and admiration in others by exhibiting a great sense of power and competency. We are surprised to find that we garner fear and respect but forgo the other, more intimate magic. Real, undying loyalty in work can never be legislated or coerced; it is based on a courageous vulnerability that invites others by our example to a frontier conversation whose outcome is yet in doubt.

We have an even stranger idea: that we will finally fall in love with *ourselves* only when we have become the totally efficient organized organism we have always wanted to be and left all of our bumbling ineptness behind. Yet in exactly the way we come to find love and intimacy with others through vulnerability, we come to those same qualities in ourselves through living out the awkwardness of not knowing, of not being in charge.

We try to construct a life in which we will be perfect, in which we will eliminate awkwardness, pass by vulnerability , ignore ineptness, only to pass through the gate of our lives and find, strangely, that the gateway is vulnerability itself. The very place we are open to the world whether we like it or not.

THE AWKWARD WAY THE SWAN WALKS

I left the doorway with whatever dignity I had remaining and went straight home. I felt as if I didn't have an ounce of energy left to do the work I had been doing. As I came in the kitchen door, I saw the bottle of red wine I had pulled out that morning sitting on the table in front of the window. Behind it, the sea formed a glinting gray green background. The dark bottle stood there in preparation for a guest I would be seeing that night. I dropped into a chair and looked at the unopened bottle and the sea and the sky for a very long time. I could feel how utterly exhausted I was in body and spirit, and how much I needed to talk with someone, anyone, but also how marvelous it was that the person arriving to share that bottle had exactly the kind of perspectives I needed at that moment.

I could see Brother David already in my mind's eye, sitting across from me with the glass of wine in front of him on the coffee table. A book of Rilke's poetry balanced on his knees. He was reciting Rilke in his rich, Austrian inflection, the sounds emanating not only from deep within his body but also from far inside some powerful understanding mediated by long years of silence and prayer. Brother David was my kind of monk; no stranger to silence but equally at home in the robust world of work, its words, and its meanings. He also loved poetry with a passion similar to my own, and exhibited a far-reaching intellect and a far-reaching imagination in its exploration. You might be impressed by his extraordinary capacity for compassion, but it did not mean he would let any unthinking assertion pass him by without a challenge or a clarification.

A few hours later, Brother David was indeed sitting in that empty chair. The bottle framed by darkness now in the window, and the cork sitting next to it. He was turning the pages of the Rilke book with one hand and sipping from his glass with the other. I had a second copy of the book but it sat on my lap unopened. After the first sip of cabernet, I felt as if I was in a deep well of fatigue looking up toward a tiny ellipse of light flickering at the surface. I felt as if the tiny light might disappear altogether and the waters flow over me if I didn't say something soon. I looked at Brother David, whose eyes had just lit up with the discovery of a poem to begin our evening, and heard him begin to read.

Diese Mushal, durch noch Ungetanes
schwer und wie gebunden hinzugehn,
gleicht dem ungeschaffnen Gang des Schwanes.

I found the poem in my own book and read, on the opposing page, Robert Bly's marvelous translation.

This clumsy living that moves lumbering
as if in ropes through what is not done,
reminds us of the awkward way the swan walks.

And to die, which is the letting go
of the ground we stand on and cling to every day,
is like the swan, when he nervously lets himself down
into the water, which receives him gaily
and which flows joyfully under
and after him, wave after wave,
while the swan, unmoving and marvelously calm,
is pleased to be carried, each moment more fully grown,
more like a king, further and further on.

—Translated by Robert Bly

I read the lines, seeing the image of the swan being borne on the waters so effortlessly, and thought of my own days so full of will and effort. I looked up at Brother David, the nearest thing I had to a truly wise person in my life, and found myself almost blurting.

"Brother David?"

I uttered it in such an old, petitionary, Catholic way that I almost thought he was going to say, "Yes, my son?" But he did not; he turned his face toward me, following the spontaneous note of desperate sincerity, and simply waited.

"Tell me about exhaustion," I said.

He looked at me with an acute, searching, compassionate ferocity for the briefest of moments, as if trying to sum up the entirety of the situation and without missing a beat, as if he had been waiting all along, to say a life-changing thing to me. He said, in the form both of a question and an assertion:

"You know that the antidote to exhaustion is not necessarily rest?"

"The antidote to exhaustion is not necessarily rest," I repeated woodenly, as if I might exhaust myself completely before I reached the end of the sentence. "What is it, then?"

"The antidote to exhaustion is *wholeheartedness*."

He looked at me for a *wholehearted* moment, as if I should fill in the blanks. But I was a blank to be filled at that moment, and though I knew something pivotal had been said, I had not the wherewithal to say anything in reply. So he carried on:

"You are so tired through and through because a good half of what you do here in this organization has nothing to do with your true powers, or the place you have reached in your life. You are only half here, and half here will kill you after a while. You need something to which you can give your full powers. You know what that is; I don't have to tell you."

He didn't have to tell me. Brother David knew I wanted my work to be my poetry.

"Go on," I said.

"You are like Rilke's Swan in his awkward waddling across the ground; the swan doesn't cure his awkwardness by beating himself on the back, by moving faster, or by trying to organize himself better. He does it by moving toward the elemental water, where he belongs. It is the simple contact with the water that gives him grace and presence. You only have to touch the elemental waters in your own life, and it will transform everything. But you have to let yourself down into those waters from the ground on which you stand, and that can be hard. Particularly if you think you might drown." He looked down and read again.

> And to die, which is the letting go
> of the ground we stand on and cling to every day . . .

He looked up again, warming to the theme. I was getting a good talking-to. "This nervously letting yourself down, this *ängstlichen Sich-Niederlassen,* as it says in the German, takes courage, and the word *courage* in English comes from the old French word *cuer,* heart. You must do something heartfelt, and you must do it soon. Let go of all this effort, and let yourself down, however awkwardly, into the waters of the work you want for yourself. It's all right, you know, to support yourself with something secondary until your work has ripened, but once it has ripened to a transparent fullness, it has to be gathered in. You have ripened already, and you are waiting to be brought in. Your exhaustion is a form of inner fermentation. You are beginning, ever so slowly"—he hesitated—"to rot on the vine."

I gave an involuntary shiver at that last image, and recoiled from the prospect. It was a prospect of an early death experienced while still alive and it jolted me out of my exhausted torpor, as if some imaginative adrenaline was now beginning to flow through my system. I looked back at him, and realized that simply in the act of coming awake for a moment, my tiredness was falling away. His words had helped to lower me deeper into myself, down into some imaginative buoyancy, had plucked me off the vine; whatever the metaphor of harvest or arrival, it was happening right there in the room. From outside the window you would have seen a younger man and an older man speaking intently over two glasses of wine, their books put aside. You would see the younger one lean forward, purse his lips, say something, laugh, and sit back again. You would have seen a moment of light intimacy; you would not have known anything had changed profoundly for the younger man in that instant. But everything had changed.

I said, "That's it, that's it exactly." I sat back. What came to my mind even as he was speaking, were the faces of all my colleagues in the organization, with whom I would have to have those difficult, courageous conversations in order to change my work; change my work more toward teaching, more toward speaking, more toward poetry. It was a daunting prospect, but I wouldn't be put off the task. I was so shaken by the moment in the doorway earlier that day and by the strong, pivotal words of Brother David's that I took those conversations as a felt challenge and discipline from that moment on. I realized I had nowhere else to go. I gathered my courage the very next morning and began to talk with my colleagues.

Over the next few months, I took the time to make those imaginary conversations real. I spoke with person after person, and slowly, conversation by conversation, changed my job description in the organization to something more fitting to my temperament. But the success itself told me the game was up for half measures. "Halfway will kill you," I remembered, as my work life slowly began to simplify and come back into focus. As I met with each of my colleagues, I began to see that in an extraordinary way the conversations themselves were doing all the work. It forced me to ask myself the next question: "If this kind of conversation will bring you the work you want for yourself within an organization, what kind of work do you really want to do in the wider world? What are your elemental waters? What courageous conversations will bring you to your poetry?" Each of us has an equivalent core in our work, whether it is the path of the artist or the explorations of the engineer. Even if we already possess the work of our dreams, there is a way of doing that work that will deepen and enliven it, a way that begs for a daily disciplined conversation.

A DAY-BY-DAY CONVERSATION
WITH THE FUTURE

I decided on two things: firstly I was going to do at least one thing every day toward my future life as a poet. I calculated that no matter how small a step I took each day, over a year that would come to a grand total of 365 actions toward the life I wanted. One thing a day adds up to a great deal over time. One thing a day is a powerful multiplier. Sometimes that one thing was writing poetry itself or memorizing lines of a newly read poem that caught my eye, or just writing a letter to an organization to say I was available for readings or talks. Sometimes it was a phone call to someone in a position of influence, letting them know what I could do. Sometimes it was preparing the ground in my mind before the conversation. Soon I felt as if I was being prepared by the conversations themselves. Over the ensuing weeks it was beginning to add up. I began to overhear a background buzz in the ethers that added to my dedication.

Second, I told everyone I knew that I was moving toward becoming a full-time poet. I wanted them to hear it and to hold me to what they had heard. Disbelief, silence, scorn, I didn't care. I was doing my damnedest to create a kind of gravitational field that would have me drawn increasingly into its center. I had an intuition that when you really annunciate what you want in the world you will always be greeted, in the first place, with some species of silence. It may be that the silence is there so that you can hear exactly what you have asked for, and hear it more clearly so that you can get it right. If the goal is real and intensely personal, as it should be, others naturally should not be able to understand it the first time it finds its own voice. It means in a way, in a very difficult way, that you are on to something. Though daunting, at the beginning, silence is good, and silence is a testing fire. There are many kinds of silence to encounter in life, but there is a particular and delicious terror to the anticipatory silence that we create from actually following our heart's desires. It seems to inflame and halo every

conversation and everything we see with a significance and import beyond the ordinary. Whether we are poets or prosecutors,
accountants or dot-com adventurers, surely what we desire from
the best of our work is a bridge to the extraordinary and a pilgrim
path to new worlds that reveals itself through a daily courageous
conversation between our own powers and the powers of the
world.

Not long ago, I heard on the radio a description of a new form
of propulsion for a probe that had just been launched into deep
space. The spacecraft was powered by a newly developed ion motor,
where sub atomic particles were propelled out the back of the
probe and provided its acceleration. The scientist describing the
new motor said that the amazing thing about the motor was that
although the electrons were pushed out of the back of the probe at
an incredible speed, the electrons were so small that the acceleration on the craft was actually only the equivalent of the weight of a
piece of paper. But because that slight weight acted every moment
and it occurred in a basically friction-free environment, the craft
could reach speeds of hundreds of thousand of miles per hour.

It is a profound metaphor for a poet, of course: just the weight
of a piece of paper, a blank piece of paper, every moment, or even to
begin with just once a day, every day. But it is a metaphor for any
work and any person. A steadily building field of activity, laid down
almost imperceptibly, layer upon layer, which creates a world and at
the same time prepares us for our appearance in that world.

The frictionless environment of space is a quality that can be
felt by earthbound humans too. We feel as if we are in a frictionless,

spacious, environment when things are moving our way and when we are engaged in a work that is our own. In that profoundly open territory we do not have to use will and effort to exert a force that will keep us going. Acceleration arises from desire itself—desire for the life we intuit awaits us. The desire itself translated step by step, day by day, into action is enough to propel us enormous distances. Once we have built our work and our contribution around our natural gifts, we have joined a great gravitational river where the current is flowing in the direction we wish to travel. Longing is a deep current of gravity that we perceive will take us home, or to a new home, and being caught in that gravity field is the sense we have of *belonging*.

Out of that gradually increasing gravitational pull, and out of silence, and out of all the actions I took in that silence, I found myself on a podium three months later, facing a very large audience, for which, despite everything I had done to arrive there, I was still not prepared. It came about very quickly, before I could complete even a quarter of those promised 365 actions. A speaker had canceled for a conference at the last moment, and one of my daily "actions" had brought me to the notice of a friend who ran the conference. From that infinitesimal but infinitely important connection, I and my work were catapulted into the visibility for which I had waited long years.

VII

The Fatal Shore:

ARRIVAL AND AUTHENTICITY

California: a misted horizon where the sea meets the sky, and from that melded horizon, white, tumultuous, rolling breakers reaching between the rocks and high pinnacles of the Monterey peninsula. Beneath you, a constant low thunder from the water, and on the beach between the promontories, a man walking the damp, undulating line drawn on the sand by each arriving wave. Beyond him the road, and beyond the road a stretch of rolling dunes sweeping toward a cluster of buildings. One building higher than the rest, a long wooden hall, crowded with people, sitting, or standing, waiting for the talk to begin.

I looked out over the assembled audience, many of them fresh from walking on the windswept beach, and felt none of the peace and tranquillity that came of walking on that sandy shore. The tumult of the waves was right here however, in the center of my chest. I was about to make myself visible, and I felt as if, true to all our old fears about coming out of hiding, I was going to pay for it. I hadn't the faintest idea what I was going to say in the talk, but two whole hours stretched before me in which to say it. An ocean of time to cross. A good part of me would rather have waded straight into the real ocean outside the hall, straight into the thunder of those oncoming waves, than face this audience, 600 strong, in this state of mind.

THE PROMISED LAND

So much of our work and our ideas of work are bent toward arrival in the promised land. We might be on a pilgrimage of identity in work, but it is almost always the prospect of arrival that keeps us going rather than the journey itself. We aim for a certain genius in our daily work which most always eludes us, but still, it is the possibility of genius that has us toiling late into the night. We aim for a marriage, a partner, a house, or a garden, and work and sacrifice for that future vision of loveliness, until sometimes the very nature of our struggle disqualifies us from the garden we have so long desired. But arrival has its own difficulties. We may imagine a place in the hierarchy of our organization where we will find safety and security, from which we will then speak out, but find ourselves just as unsure even as we pace the supposedly safe upper floor of the building. We promise to be generous with our money but die with our retirement account stuffed with ungiven treasure. We long for an audience, to be the center of attention, to have our thoughts heard in the world, and find ourselves, once it is assembled before us, terrified by the prospect.

The actual arrival at a goal always creates a turmoil unconnected to any previous imaginings. Once we cross the frontier from desire to actual fulfillment, we find that in order to inhabit the new world we have to slough off the identity that was so necessary to us as a seeker. At this point we may have become, over the years, so much the seeker that we cannot put that ever-moving, never-stopping, always-searching identity down in order to pick up anything new. We find the image of the seeker has become our ultimate defense against the intimacy of any new arrival. The promised land we thought we wanted suddenly seems to ask for a simplification of our character that seems too much too soon. Almost by definition, any real arrival always seems to occur too soon.

There is another historical reality close to the central themes of both pilgrimage and arriving. Most of the people who have arrived in a new world, in a new Jerusalem or Mecca, whether it is America, Canada, Argentina, Brazil, or Australia, found themselves, having scrimped and saved for the passage, and having been robbed blind by those who transported them, on the shore of the promised land without a penny in their pocket. It seems to be the nature of any new territory that we arrive on its borders flat broke. Any new world seems to demand dispossession and simplification. We look back in longing for our previous comforts, which, for all their smallness and poverty, at least had the richness of familiarity.

A close friend said a marvelous and disturbing thing to me one rainy afternoon. She said, looking off into the veils of gray beyond the window, that to claim our happiness in life is one of the most difficult things a human being can do. "Why?" I asked. "Because," she replied, "the moment we claim the happiness to which we have long aspired, large parts of us are immediately out of a job. All the parts of you that believed it wasn't possible are about to be let go. What is left is a simplified version of what you were before. If you do not recognize this simplified essence, you feel like a stranger to yourself."

In the allegory of the workplace, we could see my friend's description of arrival as a kind of massive inner corporate downsizing, where large parts of us then have to be retrained for other tasks. It is often the sheer scale of that simplification that scares us away from an accessible happiness and back to smaller, more complex obsessions which are at least familiar.

Whenever we are faced at last with a change for which we have looked for years, we must slip off the habituation of those same years and learn ourselves anew. I remember taking a friend, known for her grand and well-loved addictions, for a Japanese meal. She was amazed by the lightness and cleanliness of the food. "I feel so good," she said as we left the restaurant, "just as good as I when I came in. This is so unusual for me with eating," she said. "I always overdo it." She went off to bed marveling at how light she felt. The next morning at breakfast, I asked how she had slept, and with a kind of sheepish horror she confessed that she had felt so good getting into bed that she had actually been unable to sleep, as if something still had to be done and she hadn't quite got to it. She finally went to the pantry and pulled out the biggest, fattest bag of rustling Doritos she could find. Once she had taken them under the covers and consumed the whole lot, she felt normal enough to go to sleep.

There is a certain kind of heaviness and insulation we can grow used to. The body can feel strange when it inhabits the world in a lighter way, when it encounters a form of happiness or fulfillment for which it has had no apprenticeship. A lightness and litheness that gives us a sense of ease, movement and potential may bring things that have always been a struggle to us more easily, and scare us to death in the process. It may be that we felt that lightness years ago but failed in what we wanted and now the return of that possibility can be just too overwhelming. I have often thought that spending a few moments a day practicing the art of happiness, of gratefulness, of celebration and arrival, of victory in tiny but important things would go a long way toward preparing us for those grander, more lifelong goals for which we are often unprepared.

At this moment I was facing one of those grander lifelong goals. An audience for my work. A joy for which I was unprepared. It was suddenly quiet; I could almost hear the waves on the far beach if I strained. I took a deep breath as a prelude to beginning, and looked out over that beautiful beamed hall to another sea, a sea of lifted, expectant faces. They were expectant all right, expectant but puzzled. I had been brought in at the very last moment to replace a speaker who could not appear; they knew nothing about my name, my work, or anything about what I had to offer. I could understand their puzzlement, because facing them I felt completely unfamiliar to myself. I wasn't sure I had anything to offer to the audience, because not only was I in a fit of apprehension but my body felt as if it was falling apart into the bargain. I had woken just an hour before with the same exhaustion and sickness I had woken to every difficult morning for the previous week. In fact, I had been so ill for most of the conference that I had listened to the other speakers while flat on my back. Behind the last row of seats was a large carpeted area, and there I had lain, morning after morning, listening. As I listened, I watched through the higher windows of the hall, cloud line after cloud line, moving in off the sea like a mirror of the waves below, all the while wondering how I would muster the strength to stand up there and speak myself.

Exhaustion was not a good beginning for any possible future work life, and especially not as a poet. At the beginning you need verve and nerve and reserves of vitality to embark on any new path, especially to overcome any skepticism that has lodged in your own body from the outside world's refusal to believe in you. As the time for the talk grew nearer there were moments when I could have wept with frustration. For years my whole life had been leading up to just such an audience and I simply couldn't believe that I seemed in no fit condition for the encounter. I wanted badly to knock on opportunity's waiting door, but had somehow missed the street number, wandered off into a bad neighborhood, and was now knocking on death's door by gratuitous mistake. I had been given my big chance, and by the look and feel of it, I was going to fluff it. I had an audience of 600, a theme I wanted—*Entering the World of Poetry,* and the opportunity to read and recite plenty of verse, my own and others', to get to the bottom of that theme. *We must be careful what we ask for in our work,* I told myself, *we may get it,* and most likely we will not be prepared for it when it arrives.

There was another thing I had asked for, not only in my dreams, but in my waking, working, practical days: I wanted to be paid for the work. I wanted poetry to be seen as useful and practical enough that people would want to hand over a few shekels by way of happy exchange. As it turned out, they *were* paying me well, which made it worse. *Everything* was in its place, it seemed, but me. God had been good to everything except the state of the individual washed up exhausted on the shore of this promised land.

FINAL DISAPPEARANCE

My health had begun to crumble in the previous week. An uncertain weakness had slowly changed day by day to certain debilitating illness. It was over the Christmas period, and so I held off seeing a doctor. Besides, lately I had become used over the previous months to a much milder version of these symptoms. It was as if as my inner, imaginative life grew richer around my life as a poet, my outer body was sloughing and shedding itself like an outworn chrysalis. Once Christmas had passed and I had flown down to California, found Monterey, found the Conference center, and found the audience, I then found myself growing weaker and weaker and weaker. A strange exhaustion of body and spirit that had me sleeping twelve or thirteen hours at a stretch, drifting off to the sound of the waves and waking next morning almost as tired as I had the night before. It was a kind of physiological and psychological prison that seemed impossible to escape at the time, as if somewhere deep down inside me, someone had pulled an essential plug, and whatever I managed to pour in through my sleep had by morning, run right out through some invisible channel. Many of us have had a visitation of this kind of exhaustion. We look out into the morning light as we would through a barred window. Vitality is just a memory, enthusiasm is a childhood we once had.

This malady had been with me for months in a very mild form, but I seemed to degenerate quickly as the great moment approached. As the audience loomed in my mind, the merest tint of panic began to color everything. Troubled dreams and troubled days. Every morning I attempted to clear my mind for the presentation ahead, to think, to write, and to go over the poetry I had memorized for the big day, but every morning after just a few hours awake, I would find myself coasting back into an exhausted sleep. *Tomorrow I'll come round,* I thought, sure I would rally as always for the big occasion. But the rally did not happen, and the big occasion got nearer and nearer. The morning of the talk, as I woke, my heart died within me when I realized I was at the very bottom of the well looking up. I faced the light of that day with the same fear in my gut that a condemned man must face thinking of a row of raised rifles.

There was no hearty breakfast for me, however, no last wishes, and no blindfold. I told no one about my interior state; my ingrained Yorkshire inheritance forbade any complaining—where I grew up, the prospect of imminent death is no excuse for whining. But I did live in feverish wild hope: hope for a lightning storm to roll in before my talk and burn the hall to the ground; hope for a tsunami to wipe us all, audience, speaker and conference center, off the face of the earth; hope for a bomb scare, to evacuate us safely away from any dangerous, waiting, attentive crowd. Nothing happened, only the continuous arriving waves, hour after hour, heard from the beach.

FACING THE WORLD

To find good work, no matter the path we have chosen, means coming out of hiding. Good work means visibility. We have all had dreams in which we face a large audience without clothes, without notes, without an inkling of what to say; the faces expectant, waiting, terror in our eyes, the focus entirely on our lone naked figure.

Let me tell you that the terror involved in that dream is entirely and utterly accurate and most of our intuitions about the dynamics of facing large audiences are horrifyingly exact. "Just be yourself," people say, as if they have suddenly thought of something entirely original, and as if they have forgotten the terrible, wrenching initiations most religions insist on for arriving at that elusive self. To be yourself is to be no self at all but to be the frontier, the frontier between you and the audience—the large audience of a waiting crowd or the smaller more intimate audience of our immediate co-workers. Their ability to see us and know us in ways which give them a close knowledge of who we are and what we are attempting to do in the world, can seem too much, too intimate, too soon. Vulnerability and intimacy can make a very frightening shoreline. But that is a wave line we must walk in work. Work is exposure, our fancy ideas about ourselves a sandcastle built right at the edge of the incoming sea. Hence those long, nighttime dream rehearsals which have us practicing the dramatic confrontation, facing the waves, or the immensity of faces, as naked as the day we were born.

I did have my clothes on that morning, which was a slight saving grace, though at the time if I had thought for an instant that their removal might help create an interesting moment for the waiting crowd, then I might have thrown them off in an instant. Like the climactic scene from *The Full Monty,* a final blaze of poetic, suicidal, career glory, my hat spinning crazily into the astonished crowd.

I held on to my metaphorical hat, but the self-revealing nature and final uncovering I had to do, felt much the same. This was not an ordinary talk; a subject of passing interest to me. This was the core work of presenting poetry to the world, my own and others', to which I had dedicated myself. This was all of my intuitions about what I was supposed to do in life, a talk in which I was putting everything on the line; this was my work.

As I began to speak, I had a clear notion of one of the dynamics I faced. It is all very well to have a dream, but the moment you put the dream to hazard, you have the possibility of failing it. How many times do we keep a hope or a dream in abeyance because the possibility of failure is too much to contemplate? If we failed at that, then who would we be? Would there be anyone left at all? Making ourselves visible is, in effect, simultaneously arranging for the possibility of our own disappearance. I had a momentary understanding as I looked out on those upturned faces that there was no way round that disappearance, I just had to keep sight of everything that was appearing before me anew as my old sense of things disappeared. The territory that lay between me and the audience was my new home; that was what I had to focus on.

I remembered the image of Rilke's Swan from my evening with Brother David, and reminded myself that it didn't matter how awkwardly I began so long as everyone could feel me stumbling in the right direction. I began to speak, slowly and hesitatingly, but I was speaking, and the audience was listening, intrigued. All the while I carried in my mind the image of the swan slowly letting himself down into the water. I let myself down into the first poem and found a buoyancy there that would hold me. That buoyancy carried me on into the next poem, and the next. As the lines unfolded, I found myself being swept along by the currents of meaning that seemed to emerge between my voice and the ears of the listeners. As I swept downstream into the talk, the silence and spaciousness of the river of poetry began to open up a sense of rest in my own body. To my surprise, the fogginess began to clear, and to my greater surprise, I found that my groggy memory was flawless in that flow. The exhaustion began to melt away; I actually felt my hands and my voice beginning to tingle with energy and anticipation. It was if I had been holding myself completely in abeyance, squandering no extra energy at all, not even for the actions of everyday living so that I would have it all for this moment.

As I write, I think back to Cymro the old sheepdog, limping toward the back of an enormous flock of sheep, the green mountains of North Wales rearing behind him, his minute, careful movements somehow moving a whole universe of sheep along the valley bottom, without the least perceptible effort—some hidden connection working between his canine intelligence and the chaotic drift of the animals attempting to escape him. I felt the same pivotal presence with regard to all of the possible directions I could have taken in the talk and all of the possible poems I could have used. But like Cymro, battered and weak as I was, I felt I was standing in exactly the right place doing exactly the right thing, in exactly the right way.

Halfway through the talk, there was an absolute, living bond between myself and the audience, as if there were no speaker and no listener and the words were simply being created at the unknown frontier between listening and speaking. I looked out and knew this was the edge at which I wanted to live. This was the line between speech and revelation, hearing and arrival, we capture on the page and call poetry. This was my work, my water, my elemental home to which I had staggered so awkwardly and so unfaithfully. It doesn't seem to matter how awkwardly the swan moves when it is out of its element, tripping over itself on land. The arrival and grace of the creature once it reaches that water removes all blemish from the struggle to get there. I went home after the talk and resigned my position at the center.

There was nothing in my calendar, nothing in our family checkbook. There was no one, as yet, at the other end of the phone, but there would be. Before I left Monterey, I took one last walk on the misted beach. The waves were falling and crashing, rolling in from a great distance, arriving and receding as they had for centuries. I walked the tide line a very, very, happy man.

Perspectives

VIII

Outlaw Imaginings:

WHEN THE REAL YOU WANTS OUT

There is nothing stranger than success. The moment the creature arrives, it subtly alters the very work we did to become successful in the first place. Whatever measure of happiness we find in our work, once we have arrived at a goal—whether it be setting up a new business, signing up with a company, or writing a first book— it takes incredible skill not to be captured by the very structures for which we longed so deeply in the first place and which originally seemed so grand and radical. Human beings seem to have the amazing ability to turn any sudden gift of freedom or spaciousness into its exact opposite. The mantle of possibility descends upon us and instead of warming and emboldening, covers our face and our eyes. The corporate climber expects freedom and clear decision making in the executive suite and is astonished to find himself hemmed by politics, harangued by investors, and mauled by the media. The writer, finally given the advance for which she has longed for years, finds, the moment it is banked, exactly the moment she can't seem to get to her desk as easily. When she does find herself before the open page, she finds she has nothing to work against, or too much to work against. Something has changed. Before, she worked alone and her voice seemed singular and innocent. Now her writing is at the center of an enormous industry spreading out in ripples from the grain of her pine desk. She tries to create too much meaning in too short a space, or her style takes on a pleasing aspect that robs her of her original voice. She finds herself amazed and powerless; she longs secretly for the time when she went unrecognized, but she cannot send back the check, the very thing that tells her she has arrived.

The first steps into a new world reveal to us the overwhelming nature of the territory we have entered. A certain vulnerability, an ability to take risks, may have got us to the threshold, but once arrived, we may find ourselves refusing to move any further now that the outer trappings are there; we may subtly begin to circle the wagons, hunker down, drop from sight. A subtle confusion fills our nights and trammels our days, but because everyone else sees only our visibility and success, we go through the new days of arrival in an increasing daze. We long for the real, the original, the uncorrupted, but something seems to have insulated us from originality. The Greeks named this phenomena of inversion and capture *Enantiadromia:* the ability of anything followed unthinkingly, to turn into its exact opposite. Midas touches his daughter and turns her to gold. His one-dimensional ability immobilizing everything he loves to a currency that can never replace the real, underlying pulse of life.

Of course, when we first achieve a new level of mastery, a new place in the hierarchy of the great and the good, there is always a time for lying low, establishing ourselves, staying below the horizon until we find our feet. But those times tend to be shorter than we might want or think. Many newly appointed executives lose their tide if they wait too long to act. "Business as usual," everyone says, and anything attempted after the tide of expectation has receded takes twice the work and twice the convincing.

The difficult point about any sudden loss of direction, any fear that holds us back from new territory, is that we begin to think that we may be frauds, that everything that led up to this experience may have been manufactured, too. To others we are success itself, but we ourselves, feel as if we are just apprenticing ourselves again to something much larger than we anticipated. The crucial point about our arrival in a new territory is that it is often a time of disorientation, and disappearance. We look for cover as an antidote to our disorientation and disappear into the glory of our past story in the process. Our disappearance occurs at a crucial time, exactly the time when we are forming the habits and outlook that will serve us for the next stage of the journey.

The pivotal questions to ask ourselves in the mirror every morning, successful or no, are deep, uncompromising ones of personal identity. How much freedom of movement do we find now in our work, whatever the outward trappings? How much of the original person is there? Without these core questions, our great loves can turn slowly and invisibly into imprisoning forces. "I have become everything I hate," an executive once told me in the cafeteria of a large company, "yet I am doing exactly what I have always wanted to do." In his eyes I saw that he had glimpsed enormous impersonal forces for which he had no language and which, unawares, had corrupted his work, his sense of freedom, and his sense of self.

It seems to me that asking deep questions about personal freedom in work is not a selfish act, and not something aimed solely for the benefit of the person questioning. A child's sense of spaciousness and timelessness is deeply affected by the sense of freedom that their working parents possess. Any committed relationship between adults needs a mutual access to solitude that is cut off by worry, stress, or a once-successful work which now lays siege to the marriage. A child's sense of being loved is almost always linked to the parents' sense of spaciousness, and freedom, especially the freedom to be spontaneous and present.

When we try to answer questions of personal freedom in work, our first instinctual reaction can be one of powerlessness. "That's just the way it is," we say to ourselves; "that's just the way the work has to be done; that's the way the company is, the way my boss is, the way my editor is, the way my supervisor is; that's the nature of what I do, of the world in general; those are the rules; that is what I am bound by."

THE LAW AND THE OUTLAW

To preserve a sense of freedom even in the midst of rules and regulations is to preserve a part of our identities free from the strictures and responsibilities of success, career, and corporation. The measure of our continuing individuality in any work is the refusal to be swallowed by our goals, our ambitions, or our company no matter how marvelous they may be. In order to live happily within outer laws, we must have a part of us that goes its own way, that is blessedly outlaw no matter the outward conditions or rewards. A part of us that belongs to a larger world than that defined by our career goals or our retirement accounts.

The mythologist Joseph Campbell said something refreshing and radical when asked by an interviewer how an ordinary person could preserve his sense of the mythic when most feel too besieged by the little everyday claims of the bills and the mortgage. "You *must* have a place," answered Campbell, "to which you can go, in your heart, your mind, or your house, almost every day, where you do not know what you owe anyone or what anyone owes you. You must have a place you can go to where you do not know what your work is or who you work for, where you do not know who you are married to or who your children are." Hearing this, our first reaction is to believe we are being pushed toward a form of self-absorption, but Campbell's point is that most of us carry responsibility in a very selfish way, as a burden, a weight, something that diminishes us and makes us resentful of those for whom we are responsible. Campbell asks us to look for the part of us that is not beholden, that stands outside our normal structures, particularly the structures of work that can lie on us so heavily, that take so much energy to carry, and that can break the blossoming fragility of anything new and promising.

To find the roots of our responsibilities, we must go to the roots of our abilities, a journey into a core sense of ourselves where we can put together an understanding of how we are made, why we have the responsibilities we have, and, just as important, the images that formed us in our growing. We all have particular images of freedom, mischief, and radical individuality we carry deep inside ourselves which can help us to throw off the tyranny of a situation, our own indomitable stubbornness, a difficult boss, or a repressive organization. At its most desperate, the image of freedom is Thelma and Louise driving off the cliff edge; at its most integral, it can be the image of great artists, reformers, saints, or religious figures, true revolutionaries of their time, refusing to drive off the cliff edges others have so generously provided.

Most often, the images of freedom that live inside us are often images of those people who impressed us as children and who seemed to stand outside the constraining walls of the adult world. Each of us has a necessary outlaw in our inheritance on which we can call. Each of us has, in our imaginations and memories, images of freedom against the odds. As adults it may be a Nelson Mandela, the Dalai Lama, or an Amelia Earhart. As children it may have been Nancy Drew, the Littlest Hobo, or Clint Eastwood. For myself I remember the flood of sheer possibility reading about the voyages of Captain Cook in the eighteenth century, gone for years from his and my Yorkshire home, sailing the horizons of the then known world. To find these original images of childhood, we have to cross the unknown territory of our lives and reach back into our memories, our childhood bodies, and often, our childhood homes.

GOING HOME

Whatever the measure of our success, going back home either literally or in our imaginations, is such a long, long road. To return to our childhood haunts after long years away is to find ourselves in the midst of simultaneous familiarity and strangeness. We return from Vancouver, San Francisco, London, or Cape Town, or from just a few miles down the road, but the past is so immediate that it seems to speak to us like a continuous low voice in our ears. Here we shouted for our friends beneath the trees, there we fell and cut our knee; and there we bullied or were bullied ourselves, trying out the edges of power and powerlessness. We see houses exactly the same as the day we left, or the foundational outline of homes that we can now trace only in our minds. Those we knew are strangely changed and grown older, some we knew are dead and gone.

We do have our work now, a work that was formed in the growing imagination of the child we once were, but the work itself has changed and made us, formed us into something different, something perhaps good but also disturbing at the same time. We walk old familiar ways and, distant now from all the other voices that crowded our childhood, try to imagine what that dreaming young self would think of the strange adult we have become.

We may not think of the child we once were from day to day, but triggered by the deep losses or enormous gains that mark our path through life and work, we hope in secret for the child's continued friendship as we travel toward some distant maturity. Sometimes the memories are brushed aside, too painful for more than a surface investigation; sometimes they catch us unawares like a ghost brushing our wrist, a visitation of pain. Whatever memories we are able to retrieve, caught now in a form of imaginative sepia.

The child's distance from us, the child we once were, can be as painful as the distance from a real son or daughter, especially if we fear we have failed in the midst of all our public successes at a particularly private dream, a dream original to the flawed genius of our growing. Looking back to that child, we may find our earlier hopes painful; an unwanted encouragement to attempt it all once more, or, a searing memory that mocks our embittered refusal to try again.

The child's hopes for good work are centered on freedom and in that freedom, on excitement and continued possibility. The child's worst fears, seeing the continued worry on a parent's face, are that work might be entrapment after all, a cornered powerlessness and a deadly, very personal imprisonment. Desperate, the child looks for possibilities of freedom in every encounter, every person, face, and place, and stores those encounters away like buried treasure, knowing they might come to them again. To a child, a courageous aunt, a roguish uncle, an authentic teacher, a true friend; a scintillating character in a picture book, all hold, by their example, imaginative treasures that a child will use later when they must open their life and work once more to a sense of freedom and happiness. Years later, at a difficult threshold—at thirty, forty, fifty-five or sixty-five—we suddenly remember exactly the place in our body we buried those freedoms, and marking the spot, dig deep into the ground of that memory to reclaim and live them again. I have the memory of an outlaw, a particular one, that as a child I thought belonged only to my own neighborhood and my own childhood, but which I was surprised to find, growing older, belonged to the entire world.

FREEDOM AND MEMORY

From the familiar stone wall, I look across the green fields and woodlands of Hartshead. An ancient, lovely Yorkshire landscape of farms, woods and well tended fields, threaded by hidden paths I still can follow easily in my mind's eye. A landscape I know. At the brow of a hill about midway to the horizon and to the left of an immensely grand house, I see a dark smudge of trees from which the roofline of a ruined Chinese pagoda can be discerned—that is, if you know already where to find it.

Once, as a child, I stood stock-still in the forbidden and private silence beneath that ruin while two gamekeepers spoke softly on the far side of the broken wall, asking each other if they had not heard something move just then. They froze, listening intently. In the shadow of those walls, my twelve-year-old body froze with them like a ghost, an ancestral knowledge of my intrusion into the private sanctuary of the big house alive in my bones. I had the miscreant's guilt, passed down from father and mother and untold generations of the dispossessed; it fell over me as I stood crouched beneath the ruin, like a cloak of invisibility. The hands of a well-founded historic fear clamped round my throat, until I heard them go. Then I let myself escape from my immobility, dropped to the ground and ran through the woods.

I was outlaw and fugitive all at once, and watched their slowly disappearing shadows in the wood as I crept back along the path to the graveside. The grave was quiet and secluded, a place I loved, protected from intrusion, it seemed then, by its own tangible aura and by a thicket of rhododendra. A low stone wall in the gray form of a rectangle and with fallen pillars in the shadows on either side, it was capped by a tangle of rusted wrought iron, through which I could struggle for entrance, crouch by the inscribed slab, and read the old, archaic script by the dapple of wood light.

Hear underneath dis laitl Stean
Laz robert earl of Huntingtun
Ne'er arcir ver as hie sa geud
An pipl kauld im robin heud
Sick utlawz az hi an iz men
Vil england nivr si agen.

Obiit 24 Kal. Dekembris 1247

A two-hundred-year-old fake. An eighteenth-century attempt at thirteenth-century language, raised in memory of the grand outlaw of all outlaws, Robin *Heud*. It had been built by a very upper class and very law abiding gentleman whose wealth was founded on repressive land laws whose spirit that great *outlaw* had continually and repeatedly broken. But so redolent of the spirit of Robin, Earl of the Woods, was this grave, and so precise in its position in a corner of the old Kirklees Priory (where, the legend says, he was evilly and purposely bled to death by the prioress,) that it made absolutely no difference whether it were fake or no. Robin Hood's grave was an accepted fact to us locals, though most had never been there or had visited it only through the dispensations of childhood, stealing through wall and wood to arrive in the dark corner of the private enclosure for a first time, awed and astonished to discover the old script.

FREEDOM AND THE OUTLAW

As a child, before I really knew there was labor to be done in the world, or work, or responsibility, or how compelled and constrained adult life was by the necessities of providing, I walked those paths in the Hartshead landscape with Robin Locksley as a familiar presence. Not at first as a companion, but as encounter, a fleeting image: someone at the edge of the wood, glimpsed then gone, a deeper shadow on the floor of the bluebell copse, a silhouette in the slow creeping dark of childhood evenings, when I should be home. He was someone met on the path suddenly, a moment of confrontation in the eye, then away, back into history, more a haunting than a real history.

As I grew out of my childhood and began to understand that growing into the world might mean growing into a job of work, that as my young man's idea of myself became ever more focused, so did the harsh spotlight of responsibility seem to illuminate my image, I began to have a deeper sense of what had made his story and his image so abiding to me. I grew away from the child's story of *Robin Heud* and I grew and traveled away from this Yorkshire landscape, but as I grew older and came to understand more of work and the *life* of work and the way that life is contained and ordered in adulthood—how it can trap and compromise us as much as embolden and in our worst imprisonments, through overwork, create a kind of postmodern serfdom—I have grown back *toward* my childhood image of that medieval outlaw and outsider, and see him now at the corner of the path in woods, about to disappear, but beckoning me, simply by turning, to follow.

It seems to me that each of us must identify in our personal history those who represented freedom in the world, those who managed to live just outside the rules, who seemed not beholden to the forces that held others in place. I am not speaking of literal criminal activity (though, in times of war or when great individual human freedoms have been under threat the breaking of imposed laws has always been a real necessity), but of someone who seemed to exude freedom by the way they lived, who was not a slave to all the truths repeated so easily by others, who had a breath of spontaneity in their lives.

The law-abiding citizen in each of us is necessary, of course, for holding often quite precarious societal bonds together, and for stopping ourselves, when patience snaps, from doing violence to one another. We have only to look at the difficulties engulfing post–Soviet

Russia to see what happens when the rule of law is taken into the hands of business and political mafias. But in a way these were exactly the conditions that my medieval outlaw was attempting to flee. The basis of Robin's outlaw legend was that he fled the cruel sanctions of an overbearing land-owning mafia who forbade almost any activity that could better the lot of individual people. Even gathering wood from the forest to warm a cottage was often outlawed. In times of exploitation and intolerable conditions, a mere unthinking and dutiful application to the laws that create those conditions is a gospel of despair.

These medieval conditions may seem far removed from today's workplace, but we can see many parallels in the postmodern business world. There is an equivalent form of serfdom in our organizational life, except now the poverty and hopelessness lie in our lack of time and spaciousness and wherewithal to gain it back from the entities that demand so much from us in order to ensure our spending power, our promotions, and our participation. Of course, corporate entities are not abstracts working their evil way on us. We ourselves have helped to form them and helped to create them in our own image.

We are called *Homo sapiens,* which in Greek means wise human being, but perhaps, more true to our nature, we should be called *Homo forgettens,* because the capacity of human beings to forget what they are about in their work irrespective of whether they are successful is one of our great and abiding features. We can spend a third of our lives preparing ourselves for our work, and find ourselves forgetting the original inspiration behind all that preparation the moment we take a seat at our new desk.

The Greeks seemed to intuit the central importance of Memory and made her the mother of all the nine muses, implying that the nine different forms of creativity all somehow have their birth in memory. Here the Greeks were talking about memory not as *memorization* but as the deep memory of what it means to be fully human in a world that is grander than any human can conceive and more important, the deep memory of what it means to be *this* particular human being living in this particular world of suffering and loss. Somehow, whatever creative powers we have in our work are intimately connected to our ability to remember who we are amidst the traumas and losses of existence. All of our great literary traditions emphasize again and again the central importance of this dynamic: that there are tremendous forces at work upon us, trying to make us like everyone else, and therefore we must remember something intensely personal about the way we were made for this world in order to keep our integrity.

One of the distinguishing features of any courageous human being is the ability to remain unutterably themselves in the midst of conforming pressures. The surprising realization is that our friends can try to make us conform as much as our worst enemies. The excuses to fall away, to lose courage, to be other than ourselves are ever present and incredibly intimate. There seems to be no profession exempt from these warping forces, whether we are drywalling or day trading or doctoring.

Here is one Doctor Lydgate in particular, under the formidable scrutiny of George Eliot in her novel *Middlemarch*. Lydgate begins with an original approach to medicine and a strong youthful idealism, but Eliot lays out the danger awaiting him from the very beginning of Lydgate's career.

For in the multitude of middle-aged men who go about their vocations in a daily course determined for them much in the same way as the tie of their cravats, there is always a good number who once meant to shape their own deeds and alter the world a little. The story of their coming to be shapen after the average and fit to be packed by the gross, is hardly ever told even in their consciousness; for perhaps their ardour in generous unpaid toil cooled as imperceptibly as the ardour of other useful loves, till one day their earlier self walked like a ghost in its old home . . . Nothing in the world more subtle than the process of their gradual change! In the beginning they inhaled it unknowingly: you and I may have sent some of our breath towards infecting them, when we uttered our conforming falsities or drew our silly conclusions . . .

Lydgate did not mean to be one of those failures, and there was the better hope of him because his scientific interest soon took the form of professional enthusiasm: he had a youthful belief in his bread-winning work, not to be stifled . . . and he carried to his studies in London, Edinburgh, and Paris, the conviction that the medical profession as it might be was the finest in the world; presenting the most perfect interchange between science and art; offering the most direct alliance between intellectual conquest and the social good.

By chapter 76 we are witness to Lydgate's capitulation after a long grinding down; he has made a very bad marriage to a woman who has no understanding of his calling and who refuses to see his work as anything but a means of providing. After years of struggle he gives up under the unremitting pressure. Here he is confessing his fall to Dorothea Brooke. Dorothea is the epitome of integrity, memory, and patient courage in the book, so that in effect, Lydgate is confessing to an inner, former courageous self about what he feels he must do.

> *It is very clear to me that I must not count on anything else than getting away from Middlemarch as soon as I can manage it. . . . I must do as other men do, and think what will please the world and bring in money; look for a little opening in the London crowd, and push myself; set up in a watering-place, or go to some southern town where there are plenty of idle English, and get myself puffed,—that is the sort of shell I must creep into and try to keep my soul alive in.*

Most of us are rarely so honest about such an inner betrayal or the way we can make our work into a shell into which we then crawl. We are much more likely to follow the path of self-justification, adding the reasons slowly, layer upon layer, as to why it is no longer possible to live the life we desire, until our self-justifications are more real than the work itself. We might be better to look it in the face, like Lydgate, and through that honesty, unlike Lydgate, bring our powers to bear on the remedy to our sickness.

Middlemarch was written in the 1870s, but the novel speaks just as eloquently to the same work struggles of today's doctors. On the east side of Lake Washington, near Seattle, there is an astonishing concentration of wealth centered on the Microsoft headquarters in Redmond. Microsoft millionaires are numerous and an enormous part of the local economy and unfortunately, the local housing market. For many local doctors who joined the profession expecting a certain social standing to accompany their medical ideals, it has come as a rude shock to find that no matter how hard they work they find it increasingly difficult to keep themselves in the manner to which they thought they should become accustomed. Large houses are beyond their means; hourly billing is no substitute for share options in one of the mightiest companies on earth. In order to keep up the outer material life they feel is their due, many of them load their practices and billable hours to a point which their human frames or their families can only just physically bear. The money flows in but the energy in their work flows out, out of their bodies, their conversations, their hopes, and their dreams. Eventually their ideals break under the weight of social expectation. Bitterness, ennui, and self-righteousness creep in. They lose the immense sense of gift freighted in the art of doctoring itself: the daily privilege of being invited to the threshold of their patients' most intimate struggles.

This difficulty among doctors is not confined to the east side of Seattle. One family practitioner, a friend of mine, was driving on a wooded road in northern Michigan toward another long day's work, feeling the weight of the world on her shoulders; she had suddenly realized that to cover her overhead of office, staff, and malpractice insurance, she needed to bring in $160,000 a year before she could even buy herself a sandwich or a soda. She was slowly but inexorably wilting under the load, as was her sense of application to medicine; she stopped, faced up to the dynamic, simplified everything to get back to the heart of the matter, and saved her life. She resigned her position in the clinic for which she worked, moved to a smaller, slightly less imposing building, procured good secondhand equipment, shared a secretary with another doctor, and worked fewer hours. She found herself better off both financially and mentally, with more sense of repose where it mattered; in conversation with real human beings with real concerns about their well-being.

The real well-being of our person, whether it is in conversation with our doctor over the direction of our health or in conversation with ourselves over the direction of our life, is measured by a sense of freedom and spaciousness. Good health confers a sense of participation in everything around us, as does good work. Sickness is exile, in work and in play. In order to continually reimagine ourselves through our work lives, we must have a part of us that belongs to something beyond the status quo. Something over the horizon or, paradoxically, beneath us, in the ground of our life. Something as yet hidden, yet be brought to light. Something which is governed by other laws than the ones we so assiduously obey every day. Something to do with the laws that govern the way we belong to this stubborn and beautiful world.

THE OPENING OF EYES

That day I saw beneath dark clouds
the passing light over the water
and I heard the voice of the world speak out,
I knew then, as I had before,
life is no passing memory of what has been
nor the remaining pages in a great book
waiting to be read.

It is the opening of eyes long closed.
It is the vision of far-off things
seen for the silence they hold.
It is the heart after years
of secret conversing
speaking out loud in the clear air.

It is Moses in the desert
fallen to his knees before the lit bush.
It is the man throwing away his shoes
as if to enter heaven
and finding himself astonished,
opened at last,
fallen in love with solid ground.

—D. W.

God's utterance is heard from the burning bush, telling Moses to take off his shoes. "You are standing on holy ground," the voice insists. I have always been compelled by the immensity of this biblical image and have long thought that Moses' revelation was not the immediate shock of hearing God's voice from the bush but the moment he looked down and realized not only that he stood in God's presence but that he had been standing in that presence all of his life. Every step of his life had been on holy ground. The outlaw from Egypt was an outlaw because he had always felt the call of a higher legislation.

Once, after I recited *The Opening of Eyes* at a Boston reading, a Hasidic student approached me as I left the stage and asked if I knew the original translation of God's words to Moses. The question was rhetorical, and I waited with some fascination for the translation to be supplied. "The verb that God used when he asked Moses to remove his shoes was the ancient word for an animal shedding its skin. God said, '*Shed* your shoes.'"

The image seems true to me. Like most of the creatures of creation, we humans go through a periodic molt, except that our molt is an invisible one and because of the lonely invisibility of the transformation, necessitates a particular form of courage, a courage we are never sure we have in our possession. Shedding the carapace we have been building so assiduously on the surface, we must by definition give up exactly what we thought was necessary to protect us from further harm. Words will not convey that vulnerability to others; action is often inappropriate, neither can any evidence be proffered that you will grow beyond the line of your old shell. We find ourselves in the desert without food, water, or shelter. The frontier occurs in that desert, alone, the events fiery, clothed in a radical language and in a simplicity that frightens us.

> *It is Moses in the desert*
> *fallen to his knees before the lit bush.*

In a sense, at crucial and difficult thresholds in our life, the part of us that is most at home is the part of us that for most of the time has no home at all. The part of us that lives outside the normal rules. If we have no familiarity with this outlaw portion of ourselves in the normality of the everyday, then it can be very difficult to bring it to the fore when in the raw times of difficult change it is most needed.

Why are the stakes so high in our work? Why do we work long hours, ignore our children, neglect our spouse, spend enormous amounts of time away from home, and, at our worst, stoop to theft, bribery, threats, and bullying to get things done? Somewhere in the midst of work is a hidden trove of imaginative treasure that we hope can give us self-respect, independence, and the ease we desire. But to grasp any of these qualities is to attempt to touch the essence of freedom, and freedom can rarely be obtained by using methods and bully-boy tactics that imprison us by their very use. The outlaw is the radical, the one close to the roots of existence. The one who refuses to forget their humanity and in remembering, helps everyone else to remember, too.

To live with courage in any work or in any organization, we must know intimately the part of us that does not give a damn about the organization or the work. That knows how to live outside the law as well as within it. We do this not to create a veneer of protection through cynicism, but so that we can meet the powerful structures that inform our existence on equal terms, and in a real conversation of equals. In a conversation of equals, there is all to play for. Something can occur that neither side could anticipate; predictability, routinization, boredom, and powerlessness are all in abeyance. With a healthy outlaw approach, we are outside the laws of predictable cause and effect and inside the intensity of creative originality. We have a gleam in our eye; we look to the edges of things; no one really knows what we are up to. We see with the eyes of those who do not quite belong. We are dangerous again, and glad to be so.

IX

A Marriage with Silence:

ESCAPING THE PRISON OF TIME AND WORK

Our hours are numerous on this earth, but a real appreciation for most of those hours is rare. Our overemphasis on the productions of time and motion obscures the magic and spaciousness of the hours themselves, which are born again and again irrespective of whether they are worked or no. When we work only to do, we most often find ourselves helplessly doing again without having placed the first doing in any context. When doing is followed immediately on doing it can seem impossible or indulgent to celebrate any accomplishment. One set of good figures can be replaced by another on the company ledger and the bottomless hunger of Wall Street is still not appeased, the investors still unsatisfied, the media on the hunt for faults and cracks. What has been done is simply replaced by a new thing to be done; the years fly by until that strange day when all the doing suddenly has to stop; in retirement, in illness, in bereavement, in death itself. Without an appreciation of the hours of life, we are simply a target for our own incoming death, which approaches us like a missile programmed to the signature of our own fears. Living the hours spaciously, where we actually have a relationship with silence and timelessness, death is more like a difficult conversation that we join voluntarily, and in a good death—as in a good life—we have a hand in shaping that conversation.

Without the timelessness of the hours, celebration, rhythm and anticipation disappear from our work life; we lose the sense of music in our lives. As if a symphony, with all its rests, attenuated beats, and rhythms, suddenly had all silence between the notes removed, leaving the notes undifferentiated, crushed and bruised, each sound pressed into the next. Without silence work is not music, but a mechanical hum, like an old refrigerator, the white background noise corroding our attempts at a real conversation and only noticed in the reverberating kitchen, when it finally brings itself to a stop.

This perverse relationship with time is not confined to present-day life. The poet Rilke, speaking from the much quieter beginning of the twentieth century, saw our difficulties with the hours as an ancient human struggle. To give meaning to the hours, he felt, we must always give as much weight to the space between events as the events themselves.

> *My life is not this steeply sloping hour*
> *in which you see me hurrying.*
> *Much stands behind me; I stand before it like a tree;*
> *I am only one of my many mouths,*
> *and at that, the one that will be still the soonest.*
>
> *I am the rest between two notes,*
> *which are somehow always in discord*

because Death's note wants to climb over—
but in the dark interval, reconciled,
they stay there trembling,

> *And the song goes on, beautiful.*
> —RAINER MARIA RILKE
> Translated by Robert Bly

Rilke looks at the narrow human need to concentrate on the notes in music, the events of life, the foreground in the picture, until the larger canvas disappears and robs the foreground event of its significance, its rest and its breath. To find our creative powers in the time-bound world of work, Rilke insists that our inspiration is literally dependent on our expiration, strangely, on the letting go of significance, on the entry into the silence between the notes, so that the accomplishments of the day can stand against a grander, more spacious background.

I am the rest between two notes,
which are somehow always in discord
because Death's note wants to climb over—
but in the dark interval, reconciled,
they stay there trembling,

> *And the song goes on, beautiful.*

The serial events of our busy lives look very different from the perspective of the deathbed. We experience then, not clear-cut moments, but tonalities, emotional presences, the eternal spreading out in ripples from the tiny dropped stone of the remembered moment. We are each surrounded by an enormous silence that can be a blessing and a help to us, a silence in which the skein of reality is knitted and unraveled to be knit again, in which the perspectives of work can be enlarged and enriched. Silence is like a cradle holding our endeavors and our will; a silent spaciousness sustains us in our work and at the same time connects us to larger worlds that, in the busyness of our daily struggle to achieve, we have not yet investigated. Silence is the soul's break for freedom.

CREATION AND CREATIVITY

Human beings left to their own devices—a very rare event—seem to work according to the quality of a given season and learn similarly in cycles. Good work and good education are achieved by visitation and then absence, appearance and disappearance. Most people who exhibit a mastery in a work or a subject have often left it completely for a long period in their lives only to return for another look. Constant busyness has no absence in it, no openness to the arrival of any new season, no birdsong at the start of its day. Constant learning is counterproductive and makes both ourselves and the subject stale and uninteresting.

Our relationship to time has become corrupted exactly because we allow ourselves very little experience of the timeless. We speak continually of *saving* time, but time in its richness is most often lost to us when we are busy without relief. At speed, the world becomes a blur, and all those other lives we encounter that are not our own become another blur too. Our hours of work and our traveling to work are getting longer and longer, but at the same time our perception of those hours becomes shorter and shorter: short, abstract and ungraspable. We speak of *stealing time* as if it no longer belonged to us. We speak of *needing time* as if it wasn't around us already in every moment. We want to *make time* for ourselves as if it were in our power to do so. Time is the conversation with absence and visitation, the frontier between ourselves and those we love; the hours become ripe with happening only when we are attentive, patient, and present.

THE DIFFICULTY OF TIME

The commute is stop-and-go, stop-and-go, and even in the smooth encapsulation of our car we find it hard to ease ourselves into the world. We look out through the steady movement of the wipers clearing the rain methodically from our windshield and see hundreds of others, all going the same somewhere through the same downpour, and all wanting to be somewhere other than this gray no-place. We press the accelerator and surge into the next moment, but already we are stopped again, and want to be gone from all this stopping. We want to pass the car ahead, the hour ahead, the day ahead. When time is only for going and doing then our bodies are slowly bred into the perception that life and work itself is a form of commute, the whole day a traveling to and from, with the arrival rarely to be seen. The hours, we begin to feel, are not alive, but something to be filled, done with, and then discarded. When we fall to bed exhausted, we almost always rise exhausted; how we enter the hours is how we emerge from them. Just as we tell ourselves we must take time for our relationship or marriage, we must encourage ourselves to take time for the marriage with time itself.

Our marriage with time, especially in our work, is almost in the final stages of complete divorce and is the cause of as many individual tragedies as the breakdown of a real flesh-and-blood marriage. The endpoint is the same: Cast out from the luxuriant friendship and ease of the hours, we feel a blankness, a sameness, an aloneness, a lack of sense to all our doings and even our accomplishments. We attend the hushed memorial service for a dead friend and find the list of his achievements moves no one in the assembly, but the atmosphere does quicken in the crowded room when his daughter speaks of all the many things he loved and everything and everyone he held in his affections. The dogs, the chopping of wood, the homemade telescopes, the sunsets from the porch, his daughter's children, the jokes that enlivened the long meetings at work. There is laughter, surprise, revelation. Suddenly we know who we have lost, as if identity in the great measuring moment of its loss is based only on what we have loved and held in our affections and all the rest is chaff to be blown away by the arrival of death. Love is the measure of identity because in love is the timeless and untrammeled, the presence of things, the hours illuminated and celebrated like the steeple bell across the fields, filling the hollows and the hot afternoon to the brim. Death taps us on the shoulder and asks us to encapsulate a life by its loves. Death is not impressed by what we have done, unless what we have done leaves a legacy of life; death's tide washes over everything we have taken so long to write in the sand. What is remembered in all our work is what is still alive in the hearts and minds of others.

THE HOURS ARE ALIVE

Most traditional human cultures have seen the hours of the days in the same way as they have encountered the seasons of the year: not as clear lines drawn across our experience, but as an advancing quality, a presence, a visitation, and an emergence of something growing inside us as much as it is growing in the outer world. A season or an hour of the day is a visitation whose return is not always assured. Every spring following a long winter feels as miraculous as if we are seeing it for the first time. Out of the dead garden rises abundance beyond a winter eye's comprehension.

The hours and the seasons are sometimes a flowering, sometimes a disappearance, and often an indistinguishable transience between the two, but all the hours of the day and the seasons of the year enunciate some quality in the world that has its own time and place. To make friends with the hours is to come to know all the hidden correspondences inside our own bodies that match the richness and movement of life we see around us. The tragedy of constant scheduling in our work is its mechanical effect on the hours, and subsequently on our bodies, reducing the spectrum of our individual character and color to a gray sameness. Every hour left to itself has its mood and difference, a quality that should change us and re-create us according to its effect upon us.

In many traditional cultures, a particular hour of the day is seen to have a personal, almost angelic presence, something that might be named—though only in hushed tones, and only in ways that reinforce its unknowingness. The Benedictine, Brother David Steindl-Rast, defines an angel as the eternal breaking into time, each particular breakthrough of the numinous utterly extraordinary and utterly itself. Time and each hour of time is a season, almost a personality, with its own annunciation, its own song, its whispering of what is to be born in us. Its appearance like a new conversation in which we are privileged to overhear ourselves participating.

To escape from the prison of time is to grant the hours their own life; to uncurl the iron grip of our hand on any given moment while at the same time finding the ability to be more present, more robust, more open to our own self-evident absurdities, while continuing the conversation. A healthy relationship with time is an exact template of a healthy relationship between two human beings. When we make a good marriage with time, we instantly apprentice ourselves to the improvement of our character just as we do marrying another person. Not because the other person is more virtuous than we, or because we have a target personality we are trying to hit, but because whatever sanity, patience, generosity and creative genius we are able to achieve in life is not solely within our own remit. It comes from a real conversation with something other than ourselves. No matter what the New Age gurus may say, we do *not* make our own reality. We have a modest part in it, depending on how alive we are to the way the currents and eddies of time are running. Reality is the conversation between ourselves and the never ending productions of time. The closer we are to the source of the productions of time—that is, to the eternal—the more easily we understand the particular currents we must navigate on any given day. The river of time can suddenly turn, for instance, from a happy, easy flow to turmoil when, in the midst of everything, the boss asks us if we will take on a particular project that we know we cannot do with any sanity given all our present commitments; bereft of spaciousness, we say yes, trying to establish our identity through doing, afraid of the silence that might open in the presence of this figure of authority. Hounded by time, we feel hounded by others, but open to the spaciousness and silence, we can actually become fascinated by the silence that ensues from a pleasant but firm refusal. From the outside, our refusal looks like courage, but on the inside, it is simply representative of a healthy relationship with time. With regard to our marriage with time, to say yes would be the equivalent of promiscuity, of faithlessness and betrayal. Stress means we have committed adultery with regard to our marriage with time. If we want to understand the particulars of our reality, we must understand the way we conduct our daily relationship with the hours. In the hours is the secret to the workday, and in every workday the manner of our marriage to the hours and subsequently, our journey through the day, is crucial to the happiness we desire.

X

Crossing the Unknown Sea:

A VOYAGE THROUGH THE HOURS OF THE DAY

THE HOURS OF THE NIGHT

The temptation is to begin a voyage through the day with the hours of the dawn, but perhaps the workday begins where there is no day and no work at all, in the hidden hours of the night. Even awake in the dark, looking toward the shadowed ceiling, our surface sense of self unravels to a strange but familiar vulnerability. Once actually fallen to sleep, we enter a twilight world of dream where our normally controlled work personalities involve themselves with everything and everyone in ways that would astonish our waking, working friends. We wake in the distant hotel room in a confused sea of half-remembered dreams, involuntary body movements, and strange groans and noises. Our first reflection in the mirror has us searching for someone we can recognize. The person staring back at us looks nothing like the professional personality we present to the world. We rub our eyes and yawn, rejuvenated or exhausted, passionate or puzzled, slowly entering the strangeness of another day. Forty-five minutes later, we find ourselves in the conference room with all the others: calm, collected, and well groomed, as if nothing had happened to anyone, as if no one had visited this other astonishing, parallel, physically demanding world we call sleep.

We say a person *falls* to sleep as if intuiting the physical loss of control involved: the extraordinary sense of descent, of depth, and of disappearance. Sleep is intimacy and vulnerability; we define one of the ultimate human intimacies by saying two people *slept* together as if knowing that the vulnerability and mutual embrace of sleep is the defining closeness as much as the physical act of making love. In sleep, the face relaxes as it does when we die. In sleep, the underlying territory of the face is exposed, showing the innocence, the ease, and the trouble all at once, hidden under the surface toil. The presence of an innocent sleeping face causes us instinctively to tiptoe, to quieten, and to speak in hushed tones, as if the face has returned to a childhood presence whose spell could be broken by waking. Sleep is re-creation, integration, renewal and remembering, as our intuitions and increasingly our science confirms. The vast hormonal and physiological changes a person undergoes in that descent and disappearance are essential to everything in their waking day. Without sleep, without absence, without disappearance and reappearance, we lose our minds, our intellects, our sense of presence, and ultimately our physical bodies. To paraphrase Sun Tzu in his *Art of War,* when the going gets tough, the tough do not get going; they disappear, only to reappear again, renewed and reimagined.

FRIENDSHIP WITH THE NIGHT

Sleep and darkness have a primacy in our lives which is essential; yet we often see night and sleep referred to as time taken away from us, time wasted, a state only to be appreciated for what it subsequently brings to us in the following day. What would night be like seen on its own terms? Almost a third of our lives are spent in this uncontrollable, hard-to-define realm. In the same way Rilke saw silence and timelessness as qualities that were absolutely necessary in order to live well within the measured hours, he saw darkness as pure possibility and a quality which stood nobly by itself, not needing the definitions of usefulness we need in the day.

Rilke imagines a small fire seen at a distance by night, where darkness fills almost the whole canvas of vision. He realizes that even with just a pinprick of light visible in this huge expanse, we humans want to define the infinity of the canvas through that one easily referenced point of illumination. Of course, our refusal to embrace that black unknown is a function of the ancient fears we carry of darkness, and we do well to have feared it at times. Our evolutionary bodies remember the big cats and growling creatures with better eyes than ours and bigger, sharper, teeth; but Rilke asks us to reclaim the universe of the night from these old fears, to join a conversation with the not yet brought to light, and to make a friend of the unknown.

YOU DARKNESS

You darkness, from which I come,
I love you more than all the fires

that fence out the world,
for the fire makes a circle
for everyone
so that no one sees you any more.

But darkness holds it all:
the shape and the flame,
the animal and myself;
how it holds them,
all powers, all sight——

and it is possible: its great strength
is breaking into my body.

I have faith in the night.
—RAINER MARIA RILKE
    Translated by D. W.

To have faith in the night means we have a secret loyalty to things other than those that are so slavishly celebrated by all the others in the day. In the surface conversation of our colleague we listen for the undercurrent; the persistent tug and ebb that tells us she is actually going in the opposite direction to her speech. Beneath the surface of our morning commute we realize that something is taking us away in the opposite direction, that wants not just another job but another life. Watching the newscast, we realize this news is no news at all but someone else's priorities centered mostly in extremely perverse ways on the NASDAQ and the Dow Jones. A friendship with the night means we are impatient with propaganda, manipulation, advertising, the overilluminated and over-stated. We become immensely tired of hearing, from those who have no time in their own lives to stop and think deeply, that this is *the age of information.*

LOAVES AND FISHES

This is not
the age of information.
This is not
the age of information.

Forget the news
and the radio
and the blurred screen.

This is the time
of loaves
and fishes.

People are hungry,
and one good word is bread
for a thousand.

—D. W.

All attempts at spiritual sophistication aside, the man in his forties rests into an image he loved as a seven-year-old: the child opening his basket to feed the multitudes. Out of the covered night and the imagination of the night, images that are true to our struggles emerge and annunciate themselves. Amidst the plethora of information clawing at us from the insistent radio in the morning to the irrelevant television of the evening, we search for the one word that will knit sense out of nonsense. The unknown is the dark basket into which we plunge our hands to bring out words that feed the hungry and clothe the poor—as good a definition of poetry as we might find. The night is where we go to make sense of the day. Like a marriage healed slowly by a long midnight conversation in a darkened bedroom.

Night and sleep have a place in our lives equal to our attempts to control the day; we should be suspicious of all those currently boasting they need little sleep or little rest. They are by definition not to be trusted—they have no place for the unknown in them. The night sustains our humanity, our sense of ease, and our sense of compassion. Without a heartfelt sojourn in the night, the day dawns as just another box to be filled, like every other day.

To bring meaning to our day of work, we treat the night with respect, prepare for sleep as we would for anything worthwhile, enter it with awareness, leave it conscious of everything we carry from it into the heart of a day, where work can make sense.

WAKING AT DAWN

A good waking is a waking full of hearing, subtle seeing, and anticipation: the birdsong outside the house, the luminous tone of the first spring light through shutters, or the sight of a partner's face familiar and coming slowly to life again. A good waking has us listening and seeing in such a way that we are not immediately the center of the world, where we have time for the blessing of things as they are. A good waking is a spacious entry into a day where we are especially free from everything that needs to be done. Sometimes we are left thankfully alone to appreciate that spaciousness; we are the monk rising immediately and prayerfully, walking toward morning service; more often we have to struggle for it while besieged by others. The child pulls unforgivingly at our protruding leg. "Wake up, Daddy, wake up, wake up!" It's easy to be caught by the classic images of contemplation. Most parents, of course, have not taken monastic vows and for a father or mother, the first prayer is the act of paying attention to the newly woken child, to the happiness or unhappiness of their waking.

I remember being woken one morning by the cries of my three-year-old daughter, distraught by a dream, and thinking, as I comforted her, that this was just the beginning of her long apprenticeship to waking. I took her in my arms and cradled her as she fell back to a better sleep, and imagined a lifetime of wakings ahead of her: sometimes to losses that will not go away no matter how many times she falls asleep again; sometimes to the world in happy anticipation; many times to a gray sameness through which she must fight to regain her life. We should apprentice ourselves to coming awake, treat it as a form of mastery. The threshold of waking, the entry to the day, is the musician's foot lifted to begin the beat. Miss that beat and you will have to come to a stop and start again. The dash and flare of the day comes from that foot hitting the floor after the correct restful anticipation. Sometimes a prayerful, painful approach to a difficult day may mean stopping and starting a hundred times, until we learn, like a virtuoso, the thorough, attentive, rhythmic presence of the true musician.

MORNING MOOD

Waking almost always means a morning conversation with ourselves in the mirror, even if the words are unsaid and the conversation takes place only through groans and grimaces and the rubbing of our face into some form of aliveness. We greet that face again, slightly older by a day, or rejuvenated by new love or new possibility; we look hard for who is there, and gaze into the mirror as if seeing ourselves for the first time. This conversation can be comic or confrontational, or it can be deep and meditative, another prayer to set the day to rights. The following piece is a morning conversation on both the meditative *and* confrontational side of things, I wrote it as an admonition to myself.

WHAT TO REMEMBER WHEN WAKING

*In that first
hardly noticed
moment
in which you wake,
coming back
to this life
from the other
more secret,
moveable
and frighteningly
honest
world
where everything*

began,
there is a small
opening
into the new day
which closes
the moment
you begin
your plans.

What you can plan
is too small
for you to live.

What you can live
wholeheartedly
will make plans
enough
for the vitality
hidden in your sleep.

To be human
is to become visible
while carrying
what is hidden
as a gift to others.

To remember
the other world

in this world
is to live in your
true inheritance.

You are not
a troubled guest
on this earth,
you are not
an accident
amidst other accidents
you were invited
from another and greater
night
than the one
from which
you have just emerged.

Now, looking through
the slanting light
of the morning
window toward
the mountain
presence
of everything
that can be,
what urgency
calls you to your
one love? What shape

waits in the seed
of you to grow
and spread
its branches
against a future sky?

Is it waiting
in the fertile sea?
In the trees
beyond the house?
In the life
you can imagine
for yourself?
In the open
and lovely
white page
on the waiting desk?

For another person, the conversation of the morning might be completely different, involving other kinds of faith that I as an individual find neither possible nor desirable for myself; but each of us has an intuitive picture of the world and the way we ourselves were made for that world, an intuitive grasp of our place in things, which we can reestablish each morning and which can make us more available, more courageous, more generous. Each of us has the equivalent of the poet's blank page, infinite and unknown yet strangely definite in its invitation to the infinite.

This was Irish poet Patrick Kavenagh's way.

Me I will throw away
Me sufficient for the day
The sticky self that clings
Adhesions on the wings
To love and adventure,
To go on the grand tour
A man must be free
From self-necessity.

From a man who mostly wandered the grimy streets of working-class Dublin in the 1950s, there is an astonishing, lifting freedom in Kavanagh's allusion to *The Grand Tour*. To the sons of eighteenth-century British and Irish aristocracy, The Grand Tour was the finishing of a rich gentleman's education; a year among the splendors of France, Switzerland, and Italy. But Kavenagh has ennobled himself in his own imagination and sends the part of himself, poor as a church mouse but now nobly born into the world, to the farther ends of the earth.

I will have love, have love
From anything made of
And a life with a shapely form
With gaiety and charm
And capable of receiving
With grace the grace of living
And wild moments too
Self when freed from you.
Prometheus calls me on.

Prometheus calls me: Son,
We'll both go off together
In this delightful weather.

Prometheus stole fire from the gods and brought it to earth; Kavanagh has done the same in this poem and lit up the day for himself and anyone who comes across this piece of utter courage and untrammeled freedom. How we greet the dawn is a measure of the freedom we have made for ourselves. Freedom in the midst of imprisonment, freedom in the midst of all the catastrophes common to the sins of humankind, the hidden made glorious by sudden visibility; a man giving birth to himself, walking off with his new son to greet the day. Suddenly, waking from the night and the difficulties of the night; *The Grand Tour*.

THE GLAD DAY

In the old monastic day, the hours of the morning carried the Latin name *prime,* a time when work was planned, assigned, and begun. For most of us this is truly a *prime* time, when our physical bodies have the energy, the will and the vision to engage in the great conversations of life and work. One of Blake's most famous engravings is of a young man leaping out of the picture with a great blaze of light behind him, called *The Glad Day*. It carries enormous energy and youthful power, as if the youth is leaping right in our face to ask us what we are up to ourselves this glad day. The morning is the time of promise, when it feels possible to get through that pile of papers, write that memo, redo the design that has not yet turned out as it should. We are all possibility, and the world should be possibility or it dies in our hands. I remember, at twenty-one, looking dumbfounded at a letter telling me, against impossible odds, that I had won a highly prized job as a naturalist in the Galapagos islands. I was looking out of a Welsh cottage from high in Snowdonia, down the Ogwen valley, and out to the Irish Sea, holding the opened letter in my hands. I felt like the youth in Blake's painting, about to leap out of the small frame of my life.

Looking back to that younger self in the sunlit cottage room, holding the letter in belief and disbelief, I think of the remarkable qualities of that morning moment. Everyone should have at least one time in their life when they feel chosen, wanted, held up for some kind of special treatment. The times are rare, life is short, others have only a given amount of real need and generosity. It is good to be philosophical when we are not chosen, but it is a vital, precious, almost scintillating thing to be young, to be excited, to be wanted specifically for some task, and to feel a possible dream is on the edge of fulfillment. It is vital for there to be an experience of *morning* in our lives and for this experience to be called on in the memory of other, more difficult mornings to come. There is no mercy in this world if at least once in our lives we do not feel the privilege of being wanted where we also want to be wanted.

Morning is the result of two opposing currents meeting and mixing—night and day, rest and potential—and like living systems flowering into life, where cold, oxygen-rich waters meet a warmer, more nutrient-laden current, we experience life beyond the possibility of either current alone. Here is Derek Mahon, one of the finest of Ireland's contemporary poets, waking on the other side of the Irish Sea from that sunlit cottage, full of that possibility.

EVERYTHING IS GOING TO BE ALL RIGHT

How should I not be glad to contemplate
the clouds clearing beyond the dormer window
and a high tide reflected on the ceiling.
There will be dying, there will be dying,
but there is no need to go into that.
The poems flow from the hand unbidden
and the hidden source is the watchful heart.
The sun rises in spite of everything
and the far cities are beautiful and bright.
I lie here in a riot of sunlight
watching the day break and the clouds flying.
Everything is going to be all right.

Good poets don't normally go in for any form of fluffy posi-
tive thinking, so that last line is incredibly intriguing—especially
from an Irish poet who comes from a tradition where everything
has emphatically *not* been all right. You can write the line *Everything*
is going to be all right only if you have earned it by first writing.

The poems flow from the hand unbidden
And the hidden source is the watchful heart.

Derek Mahon's arrival at this astonishing, creative frontier
arises from the fact that he is all attention; he has a tremendously
watchful heart, earned probably by all the hard writing he has done
to get himself to this particular threshold and this particular morning. But the hard work leavened by the rest of the previous night and

the beauty and possibility of the coming morning makes him all arrival. At twenty I worked picking grapes in the mountain vineyards of Crete; arriving at the farmhouse at about six in the morning after a three-mile walk, I would join a pre-breakfast circle of grizzled faces, each holding a glass of intense firewater brandy; after a moment's fierce gaze at one another, we would all down the liquor in one gulp, before setting to the communal breakfast. I still can feel that spreading morning glow through my chest as I bring back the memory. Each of us has an equivalent morning draught, whether it be the aroma of good coffee, a sight of the sun, a morning prayer, or, a first hour to ourselves.

THE PRIVACY OF MORNING

Morning is precious; morning is essentially private. Morning is when we come to know ourselves in the world again. No wonder, then, that intuiting all this morning possibility, the heart sinks at the thought of meeting after meeting planned through the whole of our first productive hours.

Conversation is good; conversation can be good work; conversation is an absolute necessity; meetings must meet, but all of our verbal conversations depend on a continuous conversation with the real patterns forming in an unspoken way at the center of our work. We need this intensely personal, private conversation with what we do, or none of the other outer conversations make sense. We need the pattern made known to us again and again in intimate ways that reinforce our sense of being engaged in something real. Meetings take patience and that patience seems to be available only when we have time to understand we have a place in the much larger world that gives any meeting room its context. In work we must fight for our mornings.

There is something about the morning and morning work that demands a certain kind of aloneness, an ability to work into the day and the day's work in our own way; to find the particular contour that leads us to the particular door which opens only in a very particular way—a way which give us a sense that we are exploring the patterns emerging in our work according to our own nature and not trying to squeeze ourselves continually into an abstract box called a day or a job. Without a personal sense of investigation that a silent, spacious beginning to the day can give, we feel besieged from the beginning by everything and everyone in the office or the organization that seems to stand between ourselves and everything we have to do.

Good work takes patience, and our colleagues at work sometimes seem to need even more of our patience than the work itself, but it is hard to have a sense of ease with others when we have no time in our workday for a private encounter with the frontier of our own lives. If we have a continual sense of being besieged in our labors right from the moment we walk in the door, it is a clear signal that we lack the old hallowed office of *prime* in our work lives. *Prime* is the time to figure out the pattern, to settle into the details, to work our way into that spreadsheet, to follow the newly emerging lines on the blank page as they form into a poem. *Prime* is the time we establish ourselves in the world on individual, equal terms. Once we have contact again with an essence and a sense of accomplishment, then we can offer ourselves to others for conversation in a new way. Until then we often have little new for anyone or anything.

The morning can be make-or-break for many of us. I remember sitting silently hour after hour next to an American oil executive on a flight to Dallas from London, and the moment I said the first word I found myself in an intense conversation on the difficulties of his work morning. It was as if this time to himself alone on the plane had helped him to realize how little real time he had in his daily work. Recently transferred to England, he was having a terrible period adjusting to the open plan of his new office in central London. Not only was there no privacy in any corner of the floor, but no one had any particular desk of their own; if he arrived the least bit late there was not an inch of work space left and he would find himself wandering among the crowd until he found a corner in which to unpack his laptop. The tension of arrival robbed him of any sense of foundation for the rest of the day and any sense of sanity in his work. He found himself having to take his morning time late each evening at home, something that enabled his professional life but robbed him and his wife of the alone time they needed once the children were to bed.

PAUSE, PREPARATION, AND POSSIBILITY

How to remedy such an impossible situation? The demands of the corporation place us in a strange city with all of the cultural adjustments necessary for self and family, and then rob us of the clarity and space to do the work well. Whatever the outward conditions, it seems to me that we must not give up on the primacy of the *office* of morning because the other, actual office of work overwhelms us. Sometimes it is the physical layout of our workplace, sometimes it is the all too familiar personality of a coworker bearing down on us the moment we walk in the door. Somehow we have to find the primacy of our own experience in the midst of all the difficulty. We have to find a contour to walk, a place to stand, a wave to ride, an image from all of the many metaphors we try out that is right for us. We must find just a beginning step to freedom to open the hours of the day again. It is often a step that is both a little radical and a little rebellious. Changing our work hours; not participating in exactly the way they want us to participate; speaking out to change things. Perhaps a different form of commute that enables us to think on the train or has us turning off the radio in the car in order to take time to imagine and to plan. Perhaps a serious conversation with the overbearing colleague about our need for time to order our thoughts and our desk before we answer any questions that are not emergencies. Deep unhappiness almost always calls for deep preparation—preparation for speaking out, for changing the circumstances, for transferring, sometimes for leaving altogether. Life is too short and our work difficult enough without at least a little sense of possibility to allow the day to breathe.

There are many, of course, who go through the revolving door of their workplace, month after month, sometimes year after year, with their stomach in a knot. If the churning sense of physical unease goes on too long, they begin to associate the act of work with unease itself. Work becomes associated literally and figuratively with *disease*. The courage to leave or change becomes confused with their identification of *all* work as suffering. They feel no way out. Morning is to be feared. Work as suffering creates more suffering and initiates the slow in-breath of cynicism that begins to poison the individual acts of our endeavors. We lose the conversation with what was most precious to us and become strangers to ourselves.

SHAPING THE SELF

In a sense, each morning is a time to get to know that strange thing we call a self again and, just as important, what that self is attempting to do with its even stranger mix of selflessness, selfishness, and self-sabotage. We shape our work, and then, not surprisingly, we are shaped again by the work we have done. Sometimes, to our distress, we find ourselves in a place where the work suddenly seems to be doing all the shaping, where we do not seem able to lift ourselves out of the mud of our own making, where we do not feel able to shape ourselves at all. At this point no strategy will free us from our imprisonment, no new organizer will organize us into something new; we need time and a renewed sense of the breadth and depth of time in which to do the reimagining that is the essence of self-shaping. It is the reimagining of ourselves in our private time that allows us to then reshape ourselves in conversation with the world. I am thinking of the way the wing of an airplane is molded so that any air traveled at speed round it, lifts the wing, the plane, the passengers, and all their heavy baggage, off the ground and sustains it all through tremendous distance.

WORKING TOGETHER

We shape ourself
to fit this world

and by the world
are shaped again.

The visible
and the invisible

working together
in common cause

to produce
the miraculous.

I am thinking of the way
the intangible air

passed at speed
round a shaped wing

easily
holds our weight.

So may we, in this life
trust

to those elements
we have yet to see

or imagine
and look for the true

shape of our own self
by forming it well

to the great
intangibles about us.
—D. W.

Written for the presentation of the Collier Trophy to the Boeing
Company marking the introduction of the new 777 jet

NOON: THE THRESHOLD
BETWEEN INITIATION AND ELABORATION

However well we fly through the morning, we are cresting now toward the peak of the day, and already, as if intuiting that things have come to a fullness that doesn't entirely need us anymore, we look for a break, a lunch, a bowl of soup, another corner other than this corner in which to sit. It is time, in the order of things to let everything go so that we can pick them up again in a very different way for the afternoon. A mechanical approach to the hours sees lunch only as a fuel stop, a quick bite to keep the body going through the rest of the day. The imaginative eye sees an enormous transition from initiation to elaboration. The morning was a beginning; the afternoon is for building upon whatever beginnings we have made, otherwise we don't seem to have the energy for anything new. It's the reason we don't make important appointments for the afternoon unless we can help it. We know the person is past their best at receiving our idea no matter how much the energy of our presentation. We panic slightly if we intuit there has been no real beginning made in the morning.

We intuit the slowness of the post-lunch period even before we have taken the first bite—not surprising, as we seem to have evolved over hundreds of thousands of years taking sudden naps in the middle of the day to escape the blistering heat of the tropics. No amount of self-exhortation at this time of the day will entirely eliminate the yawning gravitational pull of sleep and the reverie of a necessary absence on our physical systems. Whether we take wine with our lunch or no, our physical prime is past its best until it recovers again for the late afternoon. Noon is always a little difficult: We suddenly feel a gnawing in the stomach, a slight irritability if the gnawing is not addressed. We look to the door or the view outside the window, ready to move away from the small view of our desk. At noon the light flattens, giving little shadow. In hot climates, the birds go silent and everything looks for shelter; but even in the busy northern latitudes, bereft of the *siesta,* we can feel a form of ennui at the center of the day, assessing already if anything really new has come from our morning. We need that glimmer of light to help us through the afternoon. Noon is the test of our fortitude and our dedication to the overall path we have made for ourselves. When we *stop* doing at lunch, we have to make some *sense* of all the doing.

FIRST THINGS FIRST

I never entered poetry in order to form a thriving business, but a business seemed to gather around my writing and work quite quickly. For many years I found it hard to admit this cuckoo in my poetic nest was as all-powerful as it seemed to be. I found myself plunging into the office first thing as if the office were my primary work. The rest of the day and the afternoon would have just an edge of panic to it, as I tried to make time amidst the growing to-do list to get to my writing. Many days the office overwhelmed me from the first moment and not a word was written, morning, noon, or night. Then an insistent part of me would secretly wonder if I were really a writer anymore or just a good businessperson living on past glory.

All this changed when I moved the office from the house, made my appearance there only after lunch at one o'clock, and gave the hours of the morning back over to writing. This morning move transformed the afternoons completely. Not only was I a writer again, but in my afternoon hours in the office I no longer felt as if I were stealing time from what was essential. For the office staff and my long suffering assistant, who all have their own morning priorities, I was certainly easier to work with. I became human again and more generous to myself and others. I was able to do the afternoon work wholeheartedly and with a sense that my main work had already been addressed. It always helps if we can arrange our work so that we do not make our colleagues into an enemy force who are out to sap our strength and steal our precious time.

The world was set to right by putting first things first; putting myself at the core of things in the earlier hours of the day, in the afternoon I was able to enjoy and give time to the secondary elaborations of my work in all its different written and recorded forms and even take pleasure in the way it was packaged and went out into the world. The world was set to right by the prioritization of the morning. At noon, we come to know how well we prioritized that morning. If we did well we know we have a wave to ride, that our work was brought to life and will give us life again for the afternoon. If we did not, we can sometimes look forward to the P.M. as a long swim against the tide.

Of course, those in structured jobs who feel there is no escape morning, noon or night from feeling besieged by their work may feel some despair at this artistic advice from a writer seemingly able to change his working hours at will. The main point, whatever our outward circumstances, is to make the morning more of our own in one way or another, to start the particular courageous conversations that will place our mornings more on our own terms, to enable the morning once again to present something of an open vista rather than an immediate besiegement. Each of us has the possibility of making tiny changes that can to our surprise make huge differences in the first hours of our work, small changes that can open up a larger view once the will is there to make the morning a prelude to possibility rather than something that frightens us back into the same corner we had left just the previous day.

In many cultures of course, lunch time is almost like an evening meal, an intense but beautiful ritual leading toward sleep and a second morning after the early-afternoon *siesta*. I remember reaching the hot noon of Crete on the terraces of the mountain vineyard, five hours of hard work after our morning brandy, ready to consume the whole contents of the massive wicker hamper the family would bring each day up the mountain. After real physical labor, a soup and sandwich will never do for the extended human system. Sitting under a tamarind tree, barely talking until the contents of the basket were laid out on the enormous cloth, I would lie exhausted, watching the matriarch of the family place on the cloth sheaves of twice-baked bread, olives, salads, tomatoes, hunks of cheese, carafes of wine, pots of snails simmered in garlic and herbs, and the dark green *dolmades,* aromatic packages sitting in their hermetic seal of grape leaves and olive oil. Once the cloth was full, eating began, followed by speech, followed by silence and the most intense visitations of sleep I can recall until I woke a half hour later looking into gnarled roots of a vine, or a face, trying to remember who and where I was.

SHARED HOURS, SHARED LABOR, SHARED FOOD

The sharing of food after the intensity of the morning work is a worldwide phenomena. The cloth seemed no smaller and the dishes just as numerous in the kitchen of the Welsh sheep farm which became my home years later as it had in the golden hills of Crete. After the communal effort of bringing in 900 sheep off the mountains of Snowdonia and sorting them out from the hundreds more belonging to our neighbors, we would set to the assembled plates of meat pies, lamb stews, salads, breads, and glorious puddings until there was very little left to be seen but scraped white china. This being the northern latitudes, there was no *siesta* unless you managed to find a comfortable armchair near to the table and did it by accident, falling asleep while the post-lunch conversation went on around you. The equivalent of the *siesta* in the north is that post-lunch talk, an easeful, enjoyable buzz if the morning work has been good, an atmosphere of contentment all the more enjoyable because you know it will come to an end—which it does when someone with the authority to do it, gives the signal to rise and move the body again toward the many sheep bleating in the fields about the house.

These are the beauties of work, particularly physical work, particularly hard physical work: shared labor and then shared food with those with whom we have worked. It is one of the great difficulties of most work today that although we may be tired mentally by the nature of what we do, the tiredness we feel in our bodies is the tiredness of inaction, of being sat too long, rather than of actual physical work. Our minds are telling us to rest, but our bodies are still dying for something real to do. Hard physical work can actually feel like a holiday activity for those of us who never lift a tool in anger during our long workdays. It is an extra loneliness to the individual when their work is so specialized that it takes an enormous amount of energy to even begin to explain to others what they do. The joy of shared physical work is also the shared tiredness, the shared hunger, and the shared conversation about all the details of the work, the aches, the pains, the tool that was sharp and worked well and how good the broth from the stew tastes.

I write this particular chapter in Ireland, on a friend's farm, high in the Burren region of North Clare, just having come in from the hard job of weeding between turnip rows. No herbicides for the organic approach of my friend. The crook of my left thumb has an enormous rising blister, and my lower back has a slight but insistent ache, showing how unfamiliar this bending work has become to me, but the seat by the fire, the pleasant conversation on turnips, of which I know next to nothing, and the physical memory of working together in the late-summer light fills me with a timeless, shared contentment it is hard to procure for love or money in any other situation. Tonight, we have been working together in time, but what we have done lies outside of time, has been done by others for thousands of years and will be done again. We have worked for ourselves but we have provided for others by happy accident: At the end of the season there will be a mound of food for all this work.

THE SHADOWS OF RETURN

As the shadows lengthen in the late afternoon, our own shadow increases and elongates with all the others. We have cast our outline against the day, and we have come to know not only the length and breadth of our achievements but also the limitations of what we can affect. In the late afternoon we begin to face limitation again, at least in our work, and the understanding that another attempt at the day is all but done. As evening approaches we begin unconsciously to assess whether we have taken another step, remained in place, or returned to familiar shadows we had hoped to God we could leave behind. Late afternoon is like the weather, changing and mercurial. It can be glowing and golden in the summer, filling the body with contentment and ease; in winter it can be just as gray and loveless, a time of midlife crisis where we transist from what the poet Gerard Manley Hopkins called the morning's dearest *freshness deep down things* to the dark inevitabilities and taboos of evening. Early in the afternoon, our prospects for the evening begin to creep into and inform the hours of work. We might have a current of calm delight running through us at the thought of dinner and good friends, or a more explosive joy that annoys our tired friends as we look forward to meeting a new love. Loveless and bereft of happiness, we may feel our neck already aching at the thought of one more lonely vigil by the television, a fleeting image of ourselves wading helplessly through the advertising for something to spark our interest. Loneliness and television aside, we may be delighted at the freedom of an evening to ourselves, reading, relaxing, and doing whatever we damn well please, thank you very much; but no matter what the surface of the later hours, late afternoon is the portion of the cycle that reminds us that everything in our work fades away and disappears. Work is not the be all and end all of human life, no matter our present obsession with its glamour and its rewards. After work in the later hours, whatever humanity we may have hidden in our work returns again for reconciliation. We each have parts of us we must face again and again, parts of us that seem inevitable no matter the surface changes attempted in the light. When the day is past its zenith, we know we must revisit those inevitabilities once more.

HOME AGAIN: THE RITUALS OF RETURN

Late afternoon is return. As the evening proceeds, we often return to family or our empty home just at the time when our best energies may have left us and our final patience expended on the traffic that dogs our commute. The late afternoon is the homeward road, but the way we enter the home can be crucial. We may have a well-loved place or a well-loved family, but we can spoil the welcome very easily by too brusque and insensitive an entry.

Living happily alone can make the entrance transition simpler: Like the monk returning to the shelter of a narrow cell we find the actual spaciousness of a palace. In the late afternoon we find ourselves naturally needing time to ourselves. Like the transitions of the early morning, there is certain important threshold of privacy necessary for the changes occurring at this late turning in the hours. Blissfully single, we turn on our favorite music, at precisely the volume we please, make tea, lie horizontal on the couch, and look round our little private kingdom. The transition can be equally cold for someone living by themselves. In periods of unhappiness we return to the bleak shadow of loneliness, desperate for someone simply to ask us about our day, for the chance to exchange and receive sympathy.

Coming home to our families presents its own possibilities and prohibitions. Intimacy with another is as hard as intimacy with the hours of the day; we forget the privilege of marriage or cohabitation, the man we fell for, the woman we wooed, when we walk through the door with our own tiredness and are presented immediately with their own competing tiredness. It is exhuasting to be exhausted and then to be presented with someone else's exhaustion. We had hoped for respite and sympathy and find ourselves having to call on reserves we do not feel we possess.

This is a moment of truth for the balance of our life and our work: How we navigate and find safe harbor in our return to hearth and home speaks volumes about the way work is arranged in our imaginations. The challenge can be immediate; *their* tiredness, we are surprised to find, is a deeper species than our own and, they seem to be implying, of a whole order of magnitude beyond our comprehension. The competitive edges can become very sharp, a couple may find themselves in the kitchen like two competing attorneys in a court of law, trying to present evidence in subtle ways to show that each of them is far more exhausted than the other. Not only that, but to their mutual rage, each feels that the other is the main cause of that tiredness and may, in fact, be wholly to blame.

Men and women often take different roads at this point to exacerbate some of the desperate dynamics of homecoming, and it is important at times to understand those differing roads. I realize that it can be incredibly tiresome to be the subject of a generalization about what men and women are like and then find that individually we do not conform to the general pattern. But if we ignore general sex differences entirely, we find enormous territories of experience closed to our insights and investigations. Men and women, *in general,* are immensely different from one another; in their modes of perception, in the way they forge their identities in this difficult world and *especially* different in their approach to conversation and the necessary conversations of work. As James Hillman has said so eloquently, women *generally* like to work face to face and men *generally* like to work shoulder to shoulder. There are plenty of exceptions on both sides, but we would be missing important and readily evident dynamics in the workplace if we pretended that both sexes approach work, conversation, or even silence in the same manner. Advances in the scientific understanding of physical sex differences with regard to hormones, brain structure, and brain chemistry increasingly point to more significant differences in the way men and women are made, rather than less. An intelligent, imaginative approach must take these differences into account without holding any one individual man or woman to a stereotype that imprisons or rejects them.

Under the stress of work, men *generally* look for peace, quiet, or even complete silence to recover. They would often prefer to sit companionably with their partner, reading or doing something shoulder to shoulder without necessarily having to talk about anything that takes any more emotional energy. A man *tends* to feel the closeness of the woman's presence as a solace in itself, out of that silence he may often ripen into conversation, (though at a pace that may drive a woman to distraction). A woman *tends* to want to diffuse the tensions and difficulties of the day by moving straight into a face-to-face talk, getting to the heart of the matter. For her this is more often an act of relaxation, while for the man it can take enormous psychological and emotional effort. Home from work he more often wants silent companionability. The goal may be shared on both sides but the way of getting there may be totally different. Once the heart of the matter is addressed then silent physical proximity may be just as nourishing to her. But getting to the heart of the matter may be the last thing in the world a man wants. For a start, he knows intuitively he is partly to blame for whatever the heart of the matter might be and that as soon as he has identified this emotional heartland, the urgencies of the masculine psyche will make him want him to do something about it or at least promise something, exactly when he is desperate to release himself from all the promises he has made in his workday. A woman may feel no compunction to action herself, the conversation being a liberating action in itself. Returning from work, the threshold encounter with another person, masculine or feminine, different or not, is a moment of vulnerability which demands enormous generosity on both sides.

VULNERABILITY AND TRANSITION

Late in our day, the first shadows of return we encounter on the threshold of our own door are times of immense vulnerability and transition. We should remember to take time for ourselves and for those who share our lives. To plan a little ahead by asking what others would like when they walk through that door, adults or children. There is no sure way of satisfying everyone but if the general needs are known, there will be at least a grand opportunity to develop a family sense of humor about what everyone is getting or not getting when they first come home. Even the acknowledgment that Dad is not getting his intimate moments alone with a chainsaw can create a laugh and a sense that a certain individuality is being recognized.

Family business can be as busy as any professional business, but it can also be a refreshing change to learn to thrive in the chaos of a full home. There are the plates, the dishes, the strange aromas, errant loved ones dashing from door to door, pets, crayons, crates of upturned unidentifiable stuffed animals and sudden teenage visitors who act as if we do not exist. Much depends on our ability to make the transition wholeheartedly from all our many attempts at control in the workplace to the happy tolerance of a family chaos that can be very good for us. The moment we enter the door from work is a primary test of the way we are attempting to make our identity through all of our hard, concentrated application. Home is where we must stop trying to control everything and enter into the conversations that humanize and ground us into the particular territory we have made our own. Home is where we stop trying to make gourmet confections refined to the precise palates of demanding customers and settle for a good hearty peasant stew thrown together from whatever is good and available: a broth that has stood and will stand the test of time, a bubbling *pot au feu* full of taste, and a dish that can be eaten happily by the most discriminating and sophisticated chef.

The tragedy of our overcommitment to work is often marked and made clear to us in these hours of return in the late afternoon. Obsessive commitment to our work, whatever fictions we tell ourselves in the office, sacrifices the timelessness of our children, the romance of our marriage, and the necessary ability to enter the sweet territory of our own solitude. The glorious and unruly momentum of our ungovernable family can grind to a halt when obstructed by our continuous anger or misery at their interference with our never-ending labors. To a man or woman under sustained stress, home can become a brief downtime of no time at all, a place they secretly resent before they free themselves and throw themselves back into the office, a place they continually fray at the edges to keep the fabric of their work whole and inviolable.

If we find ourselves angry or exhausted every evening in the kitchen, or intolerant of our spouse or our children in the living room, something is wrong with the way we are doing our work and the way that work is ultimately shaping us. What we overhear ourselves saying, as we kick off our shoes alone in the apartment or when we greet the children as we swing through the door with our tools of work folded in our bag, is indicative of our direction in life.

The voice and the identity we occupy on the threshold of our home-coming tells us whether our human pilgrimage through life is being emboldened or completely overwhelmed by our careers. Perhaps we should say overwhelmed by our *narrow* approach to work and career, because all the evidence says that the postmodern workplace is becoming just as moveable, unpredictable, passionate, human, and untideable as the average family home. We would do well to study the disciplines and art of family happiness as a template for any possible happiness in our future multi-ethnic, eccentric, and slightly chaotic organizations—organizations that will be both infinitely more ungovernable and infinitely more adaptable than we can at present imagine.

The difficulty and discipline of family life lies in the fact that we have to join the multilayered conversation on four or five levels at once, and in that conversation experience love, physical closeness, satisfaction, frustration, small griefs, and large losses, sometimes all on the same day and sometimes all at once. The difficulties of work, likewise, are becoming more and more humane; in a sense, we are beginning to imagine and commit ourselves to organizations where people will grow and throw tantrums as in any family, educate themselves, take strange paths that lead to disaster or prove us all wrong, be the cause of great profit and immeasurable expense, and eventually, like all our growing adolescents, move on and leave. For many, family life is an enormous orchestra continually rehearsing, stopping, starting, just about to begin, but never quite getting to the program, until one day, to everyone's surprise, the music stops completely, the children are gone to college, to the big city, to Africa, to who knows where, and the parents are suddenly sat facing one another in a silence that at first seems intolerable, struggling to adapt to the loss of that loving chaos.

Time flits; in the garden the shadowed gnomon of the sundial lengthens across the warm stone disk and the obsessive striving of the day has a chance to fade, asking us to give thanks for what we possess right now. If late afternoon is the time of our reconciliation with shadows, it is also the time of reconciliation with the shadows of others. There is an importance to these hours that sets our relationship with our partner or our children for the coming evening. It is important that it is marked more clearly in our minds and our imaginations. It is important that we create something timeless for our homeward return that gives everyone a chance to find their feet in the family world. A ritual tea time; for adults and children; a glass of wine for the tired couple; a time for everyone to say how everything went, or didn't. A time of truce, armistice, for the self and for others, a moment for compassionate humor, taking a breath, asking if it might be possible for so and so to happen later on, not now. A prelude for the deeper self-appraisal and self-forgiveness demanded by the final entry into night.

NIGHT AND FORGIVENESS

Night, for many, especially in the tremulous expectancy of youth, can offer sudden, glamorous transformation. Night is the time of masks, of leaving behind our daylight identities through spectacle, celebration, and intoxication. The big movie, the big party, the big game. It is dressing up, going out, putting on the Ritz of rich scents and glamours that provide us entry to worlds beyond the province of any professional work environment. The restaurant, the opera, the orchestra, the club, the clothes, the atmosphere. The boulevards of Madrid crowded with thousands until the small hours; the strip on the edge of the Middle American town, loud with engine revs, catcalls, and shouts from cruising youngsters. The glowing television screen masking and substituting for real life. Night is the time for taboo; the stretching of boundaries and edges; the illicit liaison; the hidden glimpsed, disappearing, then glimpsed again. The group of lawyers on Bourbon Street in the seemingly sin-free zone of a New Orleans night, out from the carpeted conference hall, throwing beads at women who good-naturedly offer to show their breasts. In the night we cross boundaries that our professional personalities find hard to fathom.

Night is a time of multiplicity, masks, and ephemera. The lights of the city, the hard-to-get invitation, the best table in the restaurant, the best clothes at the ball, all gone by morning, all wanted again the following night. I remember Carnival in the streets of Venice, people on stilts, fire breathers, masked eighteenth-century figures emerging from lit doorways, each person a glamorous mystery walking toward another mystery. I remember a street bounded on one side by a canal, and fifty-two people passing me dressed as a pack of cards: spades, clubs, hearts, diamonds, jacks, kings, queens. The night as a gamble, a bet, a throw of fortune. People in doorways in gorgeous sequins, standing at the thresholds of interior light, half in, half out. The night as a passage of erotic possibility.

Night lights are bright lights: the strip in Las Vegas, the Eiffel tower, the luminarios of Santa Fe. Night light is human light claimed back from the darkness of nature. We love our ability to step from the dark into light of our own human making. Out from the wind, the cold, the loneliness. Through the window of a crowded pub in County Clare, you can look from the outer blackness of a cold, Irish night and see the lit, laughing, talking faces all pressed together; the unconscious rhythm of their bodies moving to the fiddle, the flute, and the voice of the singer above the hubbub. To look in from the cold and the rain is to witness a totally different human identity than the one we inhabit standing outside, alone, on the wet road. Mostly, we go happily into the heaving room, happy and emboldened, looking forward to the music, the warmth, the conversation, and the Guinness. Sometimes there is something else we need; we stand outside and turn home for the quiet, for some form of encounter other than the involuntary one of the smoke and the crowd. Whatever the celebrations of the night, they must be lived again in the sober return of our aloneness; many times we are glad for that aloneness, but we really have no choice. It waits for us in the moments before sleep, unless we allow the oblivion of alcohol or television to accompany us right to the pillow. At the end of it all we are returned to the visitation of sleep and disappearance.

Intoxication is foundational for most human beings, a literal or metaphorical losing of ourselves, a forgetting of the self we attempt to hold together through the controlled hours of work. The Southern preacher becomes drunk in his denunciation of all forms of intoxication, leading the crowd into an equally intoxicated call and answer. Religion itself is based on the self-forgetfulness of passion, spirit, and the intoxication of the Holy Spirit. In the very middle of winter, Christmas is a lit interior made for the Christian imagination, a shelter from the cold, from work, a time for the visitation of spirits, religious or alcoholic; a time when most alcoholics are severely tested by the gravity field of intoxication surrounding them. Human beings have craved the self-forgetfulness of passionate encounter since the beginning of recorded time. The night awaits us also with its own form of encounter; celebration is for the first part of the night, but the lonely depth of the night merely bides its time, knowing we must come to it.

To forgo one form of intoxication is to hunt for another. No passion is cured without an equal one taking its place. The reformed alcoholic must find the drama of her pilgrimage back to sobriety as compelling as her initial descent into drink. She does it by telling her story again and again in the circle of listeners; her articulation finally finding a fervor that will fill her needs for self-forgetfulness.

Night still waits for us at the end of all the drama, the fervor and the celebration. The drinking must stop, the flirtation end in commitment or aloneness. The glamour and glitter of the evening grays by morning into another, less flattering picture. In all of our great contemplative traditions, the time before sleep is seen as a rehearsal for our final entry toward the ultimate transformation of death. The Christian monk examines his faults in the night office of *Compline* and sets himself the possibility of not repeating them the following day. The Zen monk taps the hanging board with a wooden mallet, while the other monks sit in meditation, chanting, *Life is a very serious matter, all things slip quickly away* . . . The period immediately before sleep is intuited as crucial even by those far from the monastery; many of us ask our children to say their prayers before sleep, though we may have long given up saying our own. Wise married couples try not to fall asleep while still angry with one another, as if intuiting the way sleep sets patterns in place, sets unspoken frustration right into our very bones.

Night and sleep is the time of summation and integration, when we work unconsciously to thread together a bedrock identity independent of work or rational thought. If we look closely at the patterns of waking, we know that we wake in almost exactly the way we fell asleep. Read into the wee hours until our eyes hurt, and we wake with the same tired eyes. Fall asleep worrying and we rise with the same residual tension following us into the bathroom. Transgress the taboos of our own conscience in the seductive glamour of the early night, and wake with that conscience howling a hundred times louder in the light of day. The pilgrimage through the night sets its direction and possibility of arrival by the way we take our first steps into sleep. The consciousness with which we commit ourselves to sleep is crucial to a good waking.

The hours of the day follow one on the other; we follow them round, cycle after cycle after cycle and then one day we come to our last hour. This last hour, if we are conscious and free from overwhelming pain, should be a time of self perspective, self-forgiveness, and, just as in the hour of sleep, self-dissolution. The deathbed is traditionally the place of confession, no matter how heinous the crime, no matter how others will judge us. We don't have the will to dissemble anymore. The pilgrimage is in its final stage. As the sense of individual self dissolves and becomes an absurd job of work that is taking far too much effort to sustain, we give up the need for cover and hiding. If we are prayerful in the transition, we might be able to find the perspective of the poet David Ignatow.

I wish I understood the beauty
in leaves falling.
To whom

are we beautiful
as we go?

What will our final perspective be on all these hours? The hours of work, the hours of wealth, the idle hours, the hours of failure and self-doubt? Who stands up and divests themselves of this body of work? Who lets go of all these accomplishments, these so-called failures? Do we look back on the wealth acquired from the acquisition, the poems published and admired, the house built and sold, the land farmed and productive, or do we see the drama of the acquisition, the beauty in the act of writing itself, the happiness the house can contain, the love of the land and the sky that nourished it? No doubt the identity we have established through all that work colors our perspective enormously. If we have built a personality through our life and work that is based on fear and keeping our nose clean, those same fears will overwhelm us completely at the precipice that awaits us at the end, until we pass over it to some other mercy beyond our own making. If we have hazarded ourselves courageously, we will be ready for the final hazarding of that depth. We will be able to look back at our endeavors with just as much courage as we look forward to giving them all up. Something was hidden in the work all along; something was hidden in our lives; something is hidden from us yet on the other side of death.

It is the hidden in our work that always holds the treasure. A life dedicated to the goodness in work is a life making visible all the rich invisible seams of existence hidden from others. Good work is grateful surprise. The value hidden in the investment, the legal case buried in the casebooks, the spare room converted and completed from the rubble of its first destruction. We must connect all this invisibility to as large a perspective as we can afford ourselves, ecologically and politically and spiritually. Whatever the hour of the day, in our work we must do the right thing, in the right way, for the right end. The multilevel discipline involved in good work is the road to happiness and the pilgrimage to self-respect. Once the job is done, we circle it, admire it—even if no one else can or will—clean up, and move on. Leaving the work to find its own place in the world is the mark of a good workman, a good workwoman. The house to be lived in generation after generation, the violin passed down, private wealth becoming inherited commonwealth. We cultivate the disciplines of care and attention in small, pivotal ways that have large, far-reaching effects on ourselves and others. Out of what is hidden we make the visible and then call it work; work that makes sense of the hours we are privileged to live.

Pilgrimage

XI

Keats and Conversation:

I have traveled to Rome a number of times in the last years. Every time I am on my way by air, sitting by the window and staring out over the very southern tip of Greenland, I clench my fist slightly, inspired by the grandeur below, and promise myself a visit to that other human-made grandeur, the Sistine Chapel. But despite my resolve I have never yet made it all the way to the Vatican. There is another, smaller chapel which entraps me on my way and holds me for the one short sightseeing afternoon I usually have to spare. The chapel that ensnares me is not really a chapel; it is only a small room, but it has the sanctity of a holy place in my imagination. It is the quiet, sheltered place where the young poet Keats died, at the age of twenty-five, in 1821.

It was quiet inside the room, so quiet you could imagine Keats's last breath, hesitating for a moment, before it finally carried him out of this world. He was young but he had already written himself into the mainstream of English literature. He has become to many, the timeless image of youth and the equally timeless representation of youthful vision, a vision that continually renews the world by looking at it with fresh eyes.

Here lies one whose name was writ in water, was the epitaph he wrote for himself. Yet despite being writ in the water of memory, his is a name that has flowed from generation to generation more alive and more distinctive every year since his death. It seems fitting then, that right outside that window, as if in another sphere of experience, you can hear a wild, happy crowd of young people gathered from all over the globe. They gather there not because of Keats's spirit but because they are drawn like he was, when he was almost as young as they, to a gathering place at the threshold between the new and the old.

Right beneath Keats's window, like a wide stone river, runs a long, branching cascade of steps. A perfect theatrical amphitheater for those below. The steps are perfect for sitting on, for observing, for seeing everything and everybody all at once, and if you look from the church of Trintá dei Monti at the very top of these steps, you can see the whole silhouette of the Eternal City against the evening sky. These steps, the Spanish Steps, as they are called, feel like the center of Rome, though they are actually on the very edge of the old city, but they also feel, seeing the sea of young faces surging over them at almost all seasons of the year, like the center of a new and forming world.

Looking down from the window you can see the young people of many different continents swaying and moving like a tide, talking laughing, watching, listening. *There is nothing stable in the world; uproar's your only music.* Keats could have been writing for our time, and if you were trying to see only what is ancient in the city, then these young people would be a distraction, but perhaps if you looked out of that window blessed with the same attentive eyes for movement as Keats possessed, you might see in them the unacknowledged legislators of our new world.

It is a sight peculiar to our epoch. There are young Italians, Americans, Germans and English, Irish and Japanese, Australian, and Malaysian and African and South American men and women all gathered in one place, sharing a distinctive worldwide music and youth culture. They are the first generation of a newly melded world that has been formed from the ashes of the old and extremely divided world, a divided world known to their parents and grandparents and to Keats himself. Many of their parents also traveled to Rome in their time, but their world had not yet melded and joined as it has for these young people. Many of their grandparents, it is astonishing to think, were trying to kill one another on the battlefields of Europe or the ravaged atolls of the South Pacific.

But this crowd has little interest in all that now. They sip from the same companionable electronic streams. Their clothes come from the ghetto streets of America or the fashionable streets of Europe, and more often than not, both at the same time. The music of their generation passes from ear to ear and antenna to antenna around the globe like a spreading electric pulse. They see and hear similar visions; they are bound together now by forces stronger than those that once attempted to force them apart. Astonishingly, for all their contemporary sophistication, they have lodged in their collective imaginations, like many of their ancestors, the experience of a parallel other world. But they do not look across the Tiber to the dome of the Vatican, or its sister religious temples around the globe, for news of this other world, no matter the beauties that the old world offers; they look to the frontiers of exploration they share through the shop windows of the world's fashion houses, the click of an MP3 recorder, or the decisive movement of an electronic mouse.

The young are wiser than we think. Keats spoke for them at this age. *O for a life of sensation rather than of thoughts!* But talk to them at any length, and many of them know, at least in a hazy way, that they are missing the depths and subtlety of the old theological order. Armani is not Michelangelo, and their two-dimensional computer screens cannot sustain their spiritual and imaginative hopes. But they also know that people such as Michelangelo were peculiar geniuses who were among the first individuals to rise above the forces of their time. Most did not. The general inheritance of their history is one of oppression and hierarchy. The spiritual inheritance was rich and deep but in those old theological and societal depths were drowned generations of individual initiative and freedom. Those previous generations had no choice but to join the hierarchies available to them; they had no choice but to join the structures available to them—join or starve, or worse. More often than not in the past, standing up to powers temporal, societal or spiritual, meant death or exile.

Even for our parents, and our parents' parents, the images of individual identity that formed and made them, were drawn from the atmosphere of the Second World War and the organizational power of military might. In North America, Northern Europe, Russia, and Japan, hardly a single adult of the war generation was untouched by the forming hand of the military, or the necessities of military production. Our corporate identities of the fifties and sixties were made in the image of those military organizations which had fought the good fight, and in the west, finally prevailed. Our organizations and our approach to work has necessarily been a product of military mobilization. But the forces that are now shaping our future are being mobilized by the individual imagination. Perhaps, more accurately, our future will come from the individual imagination in conversation with all other individual imaginations. A mobilization of something that exists at the edges between things. A sea formed not from a general's command but from the flow and turn of a thousand creative conversational elements.

Not that these young people have any special enmity toward the church—they dislike *any* organization which tries to remain a mother or a father to them beyond the span of their natural childhood, whether that controlling hand is seen in the guise of a church, a corporation or a nation state. The wish for freedom among these young people, for a life of their own, is beginning to change whole cultures. The young Japanese woman refuses any longer to be happy carrying coffee for her male colleagues. The Irish youth no longer has to live under a clouded sense of sin, emigration, and self-victimization; he looks to the celebration of a cultural intelligence that is now an international icon. The German lad does not expect to be kept in the manner to which his retiring parents have become accustomed. The young Italian woman refuses to be enmeshed in the imprisoning family drama of centuries and will not bear children. They all demand a breathing space in which they can take the time to bring their particular gifts into conversation with the life they want for themselves.

Of course we must be careful not to place all of our youth on this edge. While our late teens and early twenties are generally a time for the exploration of edges and freedom, there are plenty of the college age population, particularly in the United States, who have chosen to forgo any period of youthful wandering, and who have put their collective noses to the grindstone of corporate life very early indeed. They do not find themselves with time on their hands in the cobbled streets of Rome. They specialize early, mortgage early, and join the life of worry and concern almost immediately. They are stuck with the rest of us in the great traffic jam of modern life. They still look at prospective companies only for a combination of rewards and security. They have already, in a way, joined the older generation and have unconsciously disenfranchised themselves from any immediate reimagining of our collective future. Keats would despair at the loss, not only to themselves but to those of a slightly older generation who often, against their wills, need the noisy natural courage of youth to stir them from their learned complacencies.

The age of old complacencies, old certainties and old loyalties is over, and these young ones beneath the window represent an increasingly larger population that know it. They have what Keats described as *Negative Capability, that is when a man is capable of being in uncertainties, mysteries, doubts, without any irritable reaching after facts and reason . . .*

Our young people have negative capability because uncertainty and doubt is the nature of our time. Facts and reason are but a choice in a number of ways of looking at the world. Science is seen to have its own inbuilt bias and its own myopia, hemmed in as it is by the grant-awarding portion of a universe that it intends to understand. But those growing into young adulthood now do not see doubt as a bad thing. Not to know is the natural order of our times. To most of them, uncertainty, multiplicity, mystery and unknowing are understood as a vital way of paying attention to a new epoch forming quickly around them. They see uncertainty as a kind of breathing space from the ironbound nature of the past. To leave things unnamed is to allow them to form their own names according to the lens through which they are viewed.

We live at a remarkable threshold: for the first time in the history of the West, we have two generations in the developed world who have had a real breathing space from the last vestiges of feudalism, from the last memories of war, and from the necessities of war. Who have also, for the first time in history, a breathing space from their parental religious institutions. The church in Italy and Ireland can no longer reach its hand into the lives of young people and dominate them in the same way it was able to just thirty years ago. There is everywhere a wish for more of a conversation of equals. In Iran, the iron hand of the cleric is slowly being pried open by a generation now hungry for a life of their own. There is no doubt that much has been lost with regard to overt spiritual direction, but would any of them go back? For direction and domination? Not a chance. For a conversation of equals? Yes, perhaps.

Freedom is perhaps the ultimate spiritual longing of an individual human being, but freedom is only really appreciated when it falls within the parameters of a larger sense of belonging. In freedom is the wish to belong to structure in our own particular way. Our present obsession with the surfaces of life is at least the exploration of the extreme free end of the spectrum between freedom and belonging, even if it is sometimes a marvelous excuse to forgo the possible opposing depths of belonging.

Surfaces are part of the spirit of our time, no matter how shallow those surfaces may be. It is the prospect of freedom that we see in cars, in clothes and in music, of suddenly being alive in the world in a different way, that leads us to spend collective fortunes on them every year. We are strange, difficult creatures who long for both freedom and belonging at the same time, and often run a mile when the real thing appears. That is the frontier on which we dwell.

But perhaps, in the greater perspective of things, the instincts of our present surface loving world are correct. In a normal maturing human being, freedom allows us to make surface choices that almost always deepen into belonging: to partnership, marriage, children, or commitment to a life's work. It is as if on a grand scale across many countries and cultures, we are suddenly being left alone to explore as many surfaces as we wish and the prospect is both amazing and daunting. We do not know yet where to dig for treasure, but perhaps that will come in time. We have been orphaned from the depth of our old spiritual and organizational structures and we are refusing to go underground again until we find something freer in those depths, or until we find a newer, more spacious inheritance in which to live and breathe above ground.

Keats might have agreed with these young people's aversion to the packaged revelations of a previous age, no matter how real the original dispensation.

> *Axioms in philosophy are not axioms until they have proved upon our pulses; we read fine things but never feel them to the full until we have gone the same steps as the author.*

Keats could have been describing the hunger of our time; not the hunger for an explained meaning, but the hunger for actual experience. We want things *proved upon our pulses*. If whatever we are doing, in work or whatever we are connected to, does not prove to have a pulse or elicit a corresponding pulse in our own bodies, no matter how venerable its history, then it no longer seems real to us. History is fading from our consciousness, and we are busy forming it in our own image in the hope of making it real again. History has its pulse, and so does our own time. The heartbeat of our time has everything to do with our individual relationship to freedom and belonging.

The very confusion around what is virtual and what is real, what is advertising and what is true information, is creating a groundswell of questioning about the realities of human relationships. Without the old pressures of society and church, relationships have now become contingent more upon our instinctual imaginations. Whatever relationships we have in these times, they have to be real and vital to survive. They are contingent on the extent to which we live them out fully and wholeheartedly, to the extent to which we can instinctively imagine ourselves in them. The marriage will only remain our marriage as long as we inhabit it. The work is only our work as long it is the right work for us. A home is a home only if we can live well in it now, no matter that previous generations may have handed it down century after century. We no longer seem to have the energy for the upkeep. If we are not alive in our present home or our present relationship, it seems to be the nature of our time that they shrivel up and die around us. If it is true for the individual, it is true for our societies and our organizations. They can no longer survive as outer, hollow forms but must breathe with the life of those who make them up.

We break relationships when they are too small for us, when the home we have made in them cramps our particular style and holds us in a way that begins to deform our character. We are reimagining our houses of belonging now, and one of the first to be reimagined is the world of work. We are attempting to make work more lifelike, more in the image of what we instinctively want for ourselves.

NEW CONVERSATIONS IN THE WORKPLACE

Every organization attempting to wake up to this newly youthful world is now asking for qualities from its people that are touchstones of their humanity. *I am certain of nothing but the holiness of the heart's affections.* Keats is famous for saying. In the poetic tradition, the heart's affections are indeed holy, and if organizations are asking for people's hearts and minds, they are asking in a way for their holy and hidden affections at the same time. It is difficult to be creative and enthusiastic about anything for which we do not feel affection. If the aims of the company are entirely fiscal, then they will engage those whose affections are toward the almighty dollar. If they have a range of qualities or a sense of creative engagement to be found through their doors, they may get in return something more worthwhile from their people.

It seems to me that this contract of creativity and engagement is essential now. Companies need the contributing vitality of all the individuals who work for them in order to stay alive in the sea of changeability in which they find themselves. They must find a real way of asking people to bring these hidden, heartfelt qualities into the workplace. A way that doesn't make them feel manipulated or the subject of some five-year plan. They must ask for a real conversation.

Every organization serious about its place in this new moveable world is asking desperately for more adaptability, vitality, imagination, and the enthusiastic willingness to go the extra mile—qualities which are ancient and which human beings have wanted for themselves since the beginning of recorded history, but which they cannot give at the press of a button. None of these qualities can be legislated or coerced, they have their own life and go their own way within a person according to the elements of an individual's makeup, and especially according to the way those powers are invited from the interior of an individual to the surface.

There is no lever to pull inside a person that will activate their creativity, and no specific slogan that will bring about a passionate response. Programs are programs, and creative people are creative people, and the two do not meet happily. If there were a specific lever for all this inside them, the individuals would have pulled it for themselves a long time ago. But it is just as difficult for any individual to find their own creative powers as it is for an organization. When it comes to the moment of truth, both the organization and the individual are equally afraid of the creativity, the passion, and the courage that accompany those powers hidden within them and that are central to their vitality. This meeting place of creative anticipation and fearful arrival is the elemental core of a new conversation in the workplace.

COURAGE, CONVERSATION, FEAR, AND FAILURE

What we have to confront in the present workplace is the reluctance to engage in conversations that really invite the creative qualities hidden deep inside each human being. It is a reluctance born of the knowledge that by inviting creativity and passion, the organization must also make room for fear and failure. There is no creativity without a sense of high stakes or a sense of potential loss, and almost always, if the risk is real, then some of those potential losses become actual ones. It is a high stakes game for the company but it is also very high stakes for the individuals playing out their life's destiny within its walls. Fear loss, difficulty, failure; these are qualities and themes which make the conversation about creativity in the workplace real. To acknowledge the hidden part of human beings is to make a home for them and to create a loyalty beyond the bottom line, especially in the new territory of creative engagement into which the organization is now tiptoeing. In trying to engage people without these foundational qualities we cultivate a conversation which has no heart and no affection.

Conversation is the heart of human life and conversation is also the heart of commerce. If we take a moment to think about it, every organization must keep several different conversations vital at once. Firstly, a conversation with the unknown future gathering around their industry or their products, secondly, a conversation with their customers or the people they serve right now; and thirdly, the conversation that occurs between those who actually work together in the organization. But the depth and usefulness of *all* these outer conversations depend upon an internal conversation that is occurring within each individual. It is very difficult to make any of those outer, abstract conversations real if the people who come in through the door every day have no real conversation with their own individuality.

It is one of the tragedies of many organizations that the people placed into positions of power and leadership may have come from a technical background whose previous successes bear little resemblance to the qualities they now need. They need to be human beings attempting to engage other human beings in a conversation with the future. If our language is technical, then the qualities we draw from people will only be of a technical nature. All very well if adaptability and creativity are not needed anymore. Terribly narrow and terribly dispiriting to those who must work in technology's artificial shadow without an understanding of what it is supposed to serve. Technology's life saving and life changing gifts only make sense when cradled by a network of human conversation, a robust conversation that forms a parallel human network just as powerful as our computer networks, holding any technology to standards of sense and meaning, ethics and personal freedom.

In order to get a real conversation with the world you have to drop artificial language, you have to drop politics, and you have to drop an environment based on fear and hiding. People must be encouraged not only to know their craft, their products, their work and the people they serve, but to know a little of themselves. In order to respond to the world of *wants,* they must know something of what they *want* themselves. Just as important they must know what they *do not want.* They must also look at their inherited fears around conversation, particularly the conversation about their own gifts. This personal conversation can be very frightening but it is an increasingly necessary one, especially for those who have any leadership role in the organization.

For a real conversation we need a real language. To my mind that is the language not enshrined in business books or manuals but in our great literary traditions. Keats or Wordsworth, Emily Dickinson or Mary Oliver often say more in one line about the invisible structures that make up the average workday than a whole shelf of contemporary business books.

A New Language, a New World

The inherited language of the corporate workplace is far too small for us now. It has too little poetry, too little humanity, and too little good business sense for the world that lies before us. We only have to look at the most important word in the lexicon of the present workplace—*manager*—to understand its inherent weakness. *Manager* is derived from the old Italian and French words *maneggio* and *manège,* meaning the training, handling and riding of a horse.

It is strange to think that the whole spirit of *management* is derived from the image of getting on the back of a beast, digging your knees in, and heading it in a certain direction. The word *manager* conjures images of domination, command, and ultimate control, and the taming of a potentially wild energy. It also implies a basic unwillingness on the part of the people to be managed, a force to be corralled and reined in. All appropriate things if you wish to ride a horse, but most people don't respond very passionately or very creatively to being ridden, and the words *giddy up there* only go so far in creating the kind of responsive participation we now look for.

Sometime over the next fifty years or so, the word *manager* will disappear from our understanding of leadership, and thankfully so. Another word will emerge, more alive with possibility, more helpful, hopefully not decided upon by a committee, which will describe the new role of leadership now emerging. An image of leadership which embraces the attentive, open-minded, conversationally based, people-minded person who has not given up on her intellect and can still act and act quickly when needed. Much of the wisdom needed to create these new roles, lies not in our empirical, strategic disciplines but in our artistic traditions. It is the artist in each of us we must now encourage into the world, whether we have worked for the Getty Foundation or for Getty Oil. We must bring our visionary artistic powers into emancipation with our highly trained empirical powers of division and deduction.

THE ARTIST'S VISION

There is a good practical reason for encouraging our artistic powers within organizations that up to now might have been unwelcoming or afraid of those qualities. The artist must paint or sculpt or write, not only for the present generation but for those who have yet to be born. A good artist, it is often said, is fifty to a hundred years ahead of their time, they describe what lies over the horizon in our future world. We still have not reached the generation for which Shakespeare ultimately wrote. The artist, of whatever epoch, must also depict this new world before all of the evidence is in. They must rely on the embracing abilities of their imagination to intuit and describe what is yet a germinating seed in their present time, something that will only flower after they have written the line or painted the canvas. The present manager must learn the same artistic discipline, they must learn to respond or conceive of something that will move in the same direction in which the world is moving, without waiting for all the evidence to appear on their desks. To wait for all the evidence is to finally recognize it through a competitor's product.

There is another, more important reason. The artist's sensibility is one that grants life to things outside of our normal human ken. It understands that our place in this world can never be measured by the Dow Jones, that our ultimate arrival on our deathbed entitles us to other perspectives than mere fiscal success or the size of our retirement account. Free markets are not the be all and end all of life; they are the best we can do at the moment and are even now being ameliorated by the realization that any freedom is always understood within some far greater social, ecological, or religious sense of belonging.

In the United States in particular it is not yet understood that for the rest of the world, the conversation has moved on from the mere championing of market forces. Europe does not want hormone tainted beef, Europe and India do not want genetically modified foods, no matter the present antiseptic assurances of international scientific panels. European and Indian politicians will not be able to allow these products on the store shelves or in their fields—their peoples will not let them, no matter what they have signed at the World Trade Organization. Across the world there is a movement that is now beginning to push back and respond to the hegemony of international corporate business needs. The successful companies will be ones that do not merely lather lobbyists and politicians with buckets of money in order to keep this new world at bay, but the ones who are in conversation with this emerging alternative vision. Companies must join this conversation not only because it is the right thing to do as participants in a more and more democratic world, but also because it is a way, as Keats would have said, of *proving the world on their pulses*. The same imaginations that are pushing for a different world are the ones deciding what they want to wear and eat and watch and hear.

The young people gathered on the steps of Rome are gathered also on the steps of a new world. They are interested in a more imaginative participation than their parents can ever provide for them; they demand a different kind of conversation; they will make this world themselves no matter what we have to say. They have in their bones an understanding and a wish for more freedom—a freedom in their societies but also especially in their work. They have equality and freedom in their bones, but also a knowledge of the way individual freedoms impinge upon other people and other creatures. They have worries especially about the integrity of the biosphere. They are the first generation to look upon the sky not only as a sheltering roof, an insulation against the outer darkness, but also as a threat to their well-being. The hole in the ozone layer as yet sweeps like a searchlight each winter only over the southern ocean, but they know it is only a matter of time before its glare begins to widen. They know that the air they breathe has been changed and altered by the virtuous work of millions of others. Virtue and work for them, do not necessarily go together so easily any more. Our individual successes, they intuit, are collectively tearing at the fabric of the planet.

Keats believed toward the end that his fatal tuberculosis came from his unsatisfied love for the young woman he had wanted but left in London, Fanny Brawne. He felt as if his natural affections turned in upon himself were destroying him and bringing him to the edge of oblivion. We shake our heads, and yet we understand the allegory, and Keats did say, *A man's life of any worth is a continual allegory* . . . Our loves and affections cannot be held in some limbo inside us where they can do no harm. They are too powerful to be held in place. They want to take what they love in their arms. They have set off on a voyage from far inside us to find their home in the clear light of day, and in the intensity of that search they see opportunities and arrivals in our outer lives where we see only difficulties. Our affections and loves will not be denied but must find a home by being expressed in the world. Work is the ground of their arrival, and ours too. To die inside, is to rob our outside life of any sense of arrival from that interior. Our work is to make ourselves visible in the world. This is the soul's individual journey, and the soul would much rather fail at its own life than succeed at someone else's.

Where we find obstacles in the physical world, the soul finds a shoreline which is a frontier of arrival between the visible and the invisible. The soul of an individual is the longing inside each person for a greater sense of belonging, for a new country. We go through most workdays forgetting that this grand migratory force exists within us. We may feel a small satisfaction in a step taken, while the soul feels as if it is anchored off the promised land, with just a short row to bring it home. At the level of our souls, no matter the difficulty in our work, or the responsibilities, or the possibility of failure, entire new worlds are coming into being.

At the very end, as Keats died, his fears and regrets fell away, and the visible and the invisible became one shoreline. That far shore at the other side of life we know as death appeared and offered him a new home. As he approached this shore, his calmness and his generous nature returned. You could say that his youth returned. The vulnerable, attentive, and compassionate spirit that had written his poetry was all that was left, his true legacy. His last words were words for his friend that he should not be afraid of where he was going: *"I shall die easy—don't be frightened—be firm—and thank God it has come."*

Outside the window, the crowd is vibrant with evening and the glamour of the Roman night. The city comes to life in a new way after the business of the day. The young cross this threshold from light to dark as they must cross from youth to maturity, but for now their young eyes and ears and limbs go on watching and listening and moving happily to the invisible rhythm of their mutual anticipation. Each of their lives stretches out before them like a great journey. Each of them will look back from the end of that journey and feel their time here was as brief and fleeting as Keats felt looking back on his short twenty-five years. Keats was as old or as young when he died as any of us will ever be, because he had chanced his work in the world and won through, even as he lost his life. *I think I shall be among the English Poets after my death,* he had written three years before. None of our lives, at the end, will seem any longer than Keats's life seemed to him. At the end of every life, no matter how long or how short we compress into its span the question of our ultimate contribution. At the threshold of loss, we look back to gain a glimpse of the nature of anything we have ever held in our hands.

In work as in life, we must contemplate the loss of everything in order to know what we have to give; it is the essence of writing, the essence of working, the essence of living; an essence that we look for by hazarding our best gifts in the world, and in that perspective, all of us are young and have the possibilities of the young until our last breath goes out.

Bibliography

ACKROYD, PETER. *Blake*. Sinclair-Stevenson, 1995.

BARKER, JULIET. *The Brontës*. Phoenix Giant, 1995.

BATE, JONATHAN. *Romantic Ecology: Wordsworth and the Environmental Tradition*. Routledge, 1991.

BLAKE, WILLIAM. *William Blake* (The Oxford Authors), ed. Michael Mason. Oxford University Press, 1988.

COOTE, STEPHEN. *Keats: A Life*. Hodder and Stoughton, 1995.

DEFOE, DANIEL. *A Tour Through the Whole Island of Great Britain*. 1724–1726. Penguin, 1976.

DICKINSON, EMILY. *The Poems of Emily Dickinson*, R. W. Franklin ed., Belknap Press. Harvard University, 1951, 1955, 1979.

DONOHUE, JOHN. *Eternal Echoes.: Exploring Our Yearning to Belong*. Harper Collins, 1999.

ELIOT, GEORGE. *Middlemarch*. 1874 ed. Penguin Books, 1972.

ELIOT, T. S. *Collected Poems 1909–1962*. Harcourt Brace Jovanovich, 1963.

GILL, STEPHEN. *William Wordsworth: A Life* (Oxford Lives). Oxford University Press, 1989.

GREEN, BARBARA. *The Outlaw Robin Hood: His Yorkshire Legend*. Kirklees Metropolitan Council Cultural Services, 1991.

HANDY, CHARLES. *The Hungry Spirit*. Hutchinson, 1997.

HAWKEN, PAUL, AMORY LOVINS, AND L. HUNTER LOVINS. *Natural Capitalism*. Little, Brown and Co., 1999.

HOLT, J. C. *Robin Hood*. Thames and Hudson, 1982.

HOUGH, RICHARD. *Captain James Cook: A Biography*. W. W. Norton, 1994.

KAVANAGH, PATRICK. *The Complete Poems*. The Goldsmith Press, 1972.

PAGLIA, CAMILLE. *Sexual Personae*. Vintage Books, 1991.

RILKE, RAINER MARIA. *Selected Poems,* trans. Robert Bly. Harper & Row, 1981.

SOBEL, DAVA. *Longitude*. Walker, 1995.

STEINDL-RAST, DAVID, with SHARON LEBELL. *Music of Silence: A Sacred Journey Through the Hours of the Day*. Seastone, 1998.

TARRANT, JOHN. *The Light Inside the Dark*. HarperCollins, 1998.

WHYTE, DAVID. *Fire in the Earth*. Many Rivers Press, 1990.

———. *The House of Belonging*. Many Rivers Press, 1997.

WORDSWORTH, WILLIAM. *William Wordsworth* (The Oxford Authors), ed Stephen Gill, ed. Oxford University Press, 1988.

Permissions

Index

Index compiled by Frank Pert

FOR FURTHER INFORMATION

ON DAVID WHYTE'S WORK,

PLEASE CONTACT:

Many Rivers Company
P.O. Box 868
Langley, Washington 98260 USA
360-221-1324

www.davidwhyte.com